PRAISE

"*Sing Slivered Tongue* is a chorus of women's voices from the South Asian diaspora that speaks to the traumatic and triumphant realities of worlds severed, shattered, and somehow still surviving. This collection is an impressive contribution to the ancient traditions of women poets whose words inform not only our view of the world, but ourselves and each other through time and place."

—Kao Kalia Yang, Author of *Where Rivers Part* and *What God is Honored Here*.

"This important collection is a correction of the often forcible, gendered and cultural silencing of women's voices; the poets included recast known stories, honor victims of violence and of history itself, and share their own embodied traumas, locating strength and resilience in the intergenerational act of survival Through ruptures and fragments, metaphors and renaming, the poems gathered in *Sing, Slivered Tongue* make palpable the ways trauma, pain, and loss hold power to disrupt one's very sense of self—but also show the ways in which poetry can shine light into those fissures and create a new kind of wholeness that is simultaneously scarred and beautiful."

—Ann E. Wallace, PhD, 2023–2024 Poet Laureate of Jersey City, NJ, author of *Days of Grace and Silence: A Chronicle of COVID's Long Haul* (Kelsay Books, 2024).

Sing, Slivered Tongue

Sing, Slivered Tongue

An Anthology of South Asian Women's Poetry of Trauma in English

Edited by

Lopamudra Basu

and

Feroza Jussawalla

YODA PRESS
C-28 Mayfair Gardens
New Delhi - 110016
www.yodapress.co.in

ISBN 978-93-48566-85-0

Editors in charge: Arpita Das and Tara Mathur
Published by Arpita Das and Ishita Gupta for YODA PRESS

*To all our colleagues and friends, scholars
and poets alike.*

CONTENTS

ACKNOWLEDGMENTS

Lopamudra Basu and Feroza Jussawalla would like to thank all their contributors for their enthusiasm, patience, and dedication to this project. At Yoda Press, we are thankful to Arpita Das and Ishita Gupta for believing in the project. We would also like to thank our colleagues and friends, particularly Kanika Batra, Maryse Jayasuriya, Umme-Al-Wazedi, Shafinur Shafin, Robin Field, Gemini Wahhaj, and Khem Aryal for their help in reaching out to poets. We are grateful to Radha Chakravarty, Nishi Pulugurtha, Zilka Joseph, Maaz Bin Bilal, and Rakshanda Jalil for their advice on publication venues. We are grateful to Hafiza Nilofar Khan for her generous contribution of her artistic work for our cover and to Sonali Pattnaik, for the gift of her "Woman Reading" image. Lopa is also thankful to Kalma Ghani for her generous offer of her art, even though it could not be used.

Lopamudra Basu would like to thank her professors from Delhi University: Ratna Raman, Meenakshi Bharat, and Roopali Sircar Gaur, for encouraging her to write her poems. She also wishes to thank her friends in the Chippewa Valley Writers Guild for inviting her to participate in many poetry events. Karen Loeb, Kymberly Blaeser, Amy Fleury, Max Garland, BJ Hollars, and Nickolas Butler are writers who have made Wisconsin a home and a place for writing. Thanks to Naveen Kishore of Seagull Books, Kolkata for sharing his poems and advice on publishing poetry. Thanks to Margaret Leonard for her encouragement.

Lopa is grateful to fellow poets Jan Carroll, Jessi Peterson, Debbie Brown, Ashly Johnson, Sara Bryan and Jennifer Eddy. This group of women who are the Poets of the Oak Lair have been a source of inspiration and encouragement. Among her colleagues at University of Wisconsin-Stout, Lopa would like to thank Kevin Drzakowski, Jeremiah Bass, Daniel Ruefman, Kristin Risley, Julie Watts, Mary Climes, and Andrew Cochran for their enthusiasm in organizing many local poetry readings. She is thankful to UW-Stout librarians Cory Mitchell and Cory Whipkey for their help in locating research materials.

Lopa is very grateful for the support of her family. Her mother Jayasree Bhattacharjee, sister Jayeeta Bose, nieces Sharanya and

Srina continue to inspire her. Thanks to Purabi Panwar for her advice on publishers. At her home in Wisconsin, this work could not have been accomplished without the support of her husband Sandeep and son Aviroop Basu. She is especially thankful to Avi for his help with technical assistance. She is thankful to her friend Dr. Sanjukta Dey of Kolkata for being a reader of her poetry from grade school to midlife.

Feroza would like to thank her cheerleaders, particularly Dr. Kanika Batra, Dr. Manav Ratti, Dr. Om P. Dwivedi for continuous positive encouragement. Feroza would like to thank Lopa Basu for bringing her onto this project and doing all the hard work in putting this volume together!

Finally, both Feroza and Lopa would like to thank Andrew Fields for his diligence and care with the manuscript.

INTRODUCTION

Poetry and Trauma

Our anthology of poetry, featuring well-known and emerging poets, breaks new ground in two major ways. First, our volume is devoted to women's writing on trauma. We believe a book with this thematic focus distinguishes our collection from other contemporary anthologies. Second, we are committed to a transnational vision of South Asia, one that is not limited to national boundaries but includes poets from South Asian nations and its varied diasporic communities. In this introductory essay, we reflect on the relationship between trauma, memory, and poetic expression. It is our attempt to give voice to many buried and repressed experiences of women. We also trace the inspiration for our work in South Asian poetic traditions, historically, as well as among specific poets whose earlier work paved the way for our current project. This introduction is not exhaustive, but we hope it will orient readers to common thematic and stylistic threads that unify this work.

South Asian women's poetry in English gives voice to trauma and loss, in order to effect change and ensure that the cries of trauma are heard. Trauma, particularly that of women, has typically been relegated to silence and oblivion. This is why we have titled our collection of poems *Sing Slivered Tongue*, recalling the myth of Khona whose tongue was slivered because she attempted to speak. Radha Chakravarty's poem "Severed Tongue," included in this volume, draws on this myth of Khona, the famous ancient Indian woman astrologer whose prophecies were astonishingly accurate, but who, due to the jealousy of male colleagues, had her tongue slivered so she could speak no more. Laksmisree Banerjee's poem "I Grow in Death," also invokes the image of a woman's severed tongue. Roopali Sircar Gaur turns to the Greek myth of Philomela to address the silencing of women in the aftermath of horrific gangrapes and abuse. Like Shakespeare's Gertrude who urges Hamlet not to speak any more as he bares his chest too much, women were urged to speak no more as they bared their chests. Gayatri Chakravarty Spivak in her famous essay "Can the Subaltern Speak?" had argued that the subaltern cannot speak. The information gathered by many feminist intellectuals of subaltern women ultimately produces "epistemic violence. . . and the subaltern will be as mute as ever" (Spivak 90). In this collection of poetry, we give voice to the outpourings of women speaking trauma from death, disaster, divorces, separations, and political marginalizations. Yet, we are cognizant that we are still distanced from the subaltern, and we cannot capture the traumas affecting those most disenfranchised. In the midst of these poetic expressions, we acknowledge trauma that cannot find expression in language.

South Asian poetry in English, especially that written by South Asian women, is the "Mother" of South Asian Literature in English. This statement may seem to be contradictory to the relative marginality of poetry in the market of South Asian literature and world literature in general. While South Asian novelists like Salman Rushdie, Arundhati Roy, Jhumpa Lahiri and most recently V.V. Ganeshananthan have become household names winning the Booker, Pulitzer and the Carol Shields prizes (Ganeshananthan), poetry has remained a minor genre struggling to gain visibility and often shunned by readers for its perceived difficulty.

The introduction to Basu and Leenerts's *Passage to Manhattan* (2009) explores the problem of poetry's marginality through the lens of Jahan Ramazani's book *The Hybrid Muse* (2001), in which he argued that poetry had been neglected in the field of postcolonial literature because novels afford a mimetic framework of reading representations of the societies they originate from. Poetry, Ramazani argued, "is harder to annex as textual synecdoche" (Ramazani 4). It is precisely because poetry does not offer a mimetic, one-to-one correspondence with social realities that it enables more subtle, surprising, and nuanced responses to the multiple realities of contemporary postcolonial societies, especially in South Asia. This is seen in collections such as *I am Rohingya: Poetry from the Camps and Beyond*, edited by James Byrne and Shehzar Doja which was an example of a project that lent itself to the expression of trauma through poetic testimonies of Rohingya refugees in camps. In his book, *Poetry as Testimony: Witnessing and Memory in Twentieth Century Poems*, Antony Rowland follows the lead of trauma theorists Shoshana Felman and Dori Laub and argues about the special place of poetry as a genre of testimony. Unlike legal testimony prepared for courts to document and seek redress for atrocities, poetic testimony "does not comprise of a mimetic reflection of the experience but the re inscription of trauma in literary form. . ." (Rowland 11) However, even in Byrne and Doja's *I am Rohingya*, women's experiences are not directly accessible. Women in the Rohingya refugee camps did not participate in the writing workshops due to cultural barriers in women accessing public spaces.

Keeping such issues of women's invisibility and silencing in mind, our project enables us to bring our scholarly and creative pursuits to a productive synthesis. We also hope that we are contributing in bringing not only established but various emerging poets together in this volume, making it a resource for those who wish to teach South Asian women's literature and would like to explore genres beyond prose.

It is useful to generate a definition of trauma in this introductory essay before we explore the different kinds of trauma that our collection includes. Lucy Bond and Stef Craps in their book *Trauma* in the Routledge New Critical Idiom series write that "most cultural and literary theories position trauma as a *belated* response to an overwhelming event too shattering to be processed as it occurs" (4). They elaborate further that "Trauma, then is slippery, blurring the boundaries between mind and body, memory and forgetting. speech and silence" (Bond and Craps, 5). In an earlier essay titled "Beyond Eurocentrism: Trauma Theory in the Global Age," Stef Craps had argued that trauma theorists originating in many cases from the western world seem to perpetuate a sense of asymmetry of grief experienced in different locations. Craps argues that instead of trauma uniting cultures, there is a Eurocentric bias in privileging some historical traumas more than others. It is with a view of correcting this neglect that our volume focuses on traumas depicted by South Asian women poets. Gautam Karmakar and Zeenat Khan in their book *Narratives of Trauma in South Asian Literature* acknowledge the work of Craps and Bond, explaining their own project as the "study of unrecognized and unaddressed traumatic narratives from South Asia . . ." (9). They go on to argue that literary works from South Asia "document the psychological trauma of South Asians that has not been registered in the historical chronicles" (11). Our book is an attempt to respond to this vacuum by curating poems of trauma by South Asian women in South Asian nations and diasporic communities

Pramod K. Nayar has given us a useful structure for understanding trauma in the South Asian context. He provides a framework for understanding such issues as affirmative action for "Dalits and disempowered groups," domestic violence, and the lives of sex workers. Nayar asserts that "Trauma serves as a useful critical conceptual category for analyzing women's writing and experience, even when the victims (or survivors) belong to different social and economic classes" (28). Nayar claims that it is not his intention "to elide such crucial class and social differences" (ibid.) but he wants to identify a common register of trauma. The purpose is to respond to trauma through the discourse of universal human rights. We believe that our project, although confined to the genre of poetry and its more indirect and often symbolic acts of bearing witness to trauma, is still pursuing the task of creating a public culture of engagement with women's trauma, which has been largely invisible and unrecorded.

Another question that we wish to address is why we have chosen to limit ourselves to the traumatic experiences of South Asian women. First, we do not think of women as a category based only on biological attributes. In a time of gender fluidity, we recognize that women are socially constructed, and we are inclusive of those who were born into that identity and those who chose this gender to define their gender identity. Do South Asian men not experience trauma and why have we not included them in our volume? We focus on South Asian women's poetry of trauma because this is an experience that has not garnered enough visibility. In South Asian history, trauma is often experienced in a gendered manner. Historically, the 1947 Partition and the 1971 Bangladesh War of Liberation were particularly traumatic for women who experienced sexual violence on their bodies. These experiences were largely repressed and consigned to silence. It is only after the passage of many decades that scholars like Urvashi Butalia, Ritu Menon, and Kamla Bhasin attempted to retrieve and collect these memories and oral histories of women. These projects paralleled renewed interest in the 1980s and 1990s in creative writing about Partition trauma by writers like Bapsi Sidhwa and Shauna Singh Baldwin, many decades after the original violent events.

This reiterates the belated and recursive nature of trauma. In the Sri Lankan Civil War, which began in the 1980s and continued for three decades, we experienced again the vulnerability of women's bodies in ethnic conflicts. Tamil women got recruited to become suicide bombers sacrificing their bodies to the cause of a Tamil homeland. They were also often at the receiving end of sexual violence from the Indian Peacekeeping Force. Even though this war is over, its memory continues to haunt the fragile nation.

We are aware of the danger of ghettoization of women poets which Rosinka Chowdhury warned us about in her introduction to *A History of Indian Poetry in English*. She made the choice of not putting women poets in a "separate fenced enclosure" (Chowdhury 14) in her book. However, we believe the time is now ripe for more space to be allotted to women poets, in the light of various urgent issues facing them. In contemporary South Asian communities, trauma takes the form of climate insecurity, fragility of family structures, financial precarity in an age of globalization, and the experience of encountering racism in new diasporic locations. Our decision to focus on South Asian women's poetry seems particularly relevant to the times we are living in.

The vulnerability of women to sexual violence was witnessed in the infamous Nirbhaya rape case, when a young woman was brutally gangraped and killed in a Delhi bus in 2012. This incident, coming in the wake of many instances of sexual violence in India perpetrated on women, galvanized a nation to protest and demand justice for rape victims. Yet even though the adult rapists were given the death penalty in this case, sexual violence still goes unpunished in India. In 2020, in Hathras, a Dalit woman was gangraped, her tongue mutilated, (a perfect literal example of why we chose the title), her spine broken before she was killed, yet her murderers were not brought to justice. The Kathua case in 2018 involved the gangrape and murder of an eight-year-old child, Asifa Bano. All these cases highlight the continuing vulnerabilities of women in India. Of course, other facets of social and economic identity like caste and minority status greatly exacerbate these threats.

This precarity of women's rights is also being experienced in South Asian diasporic communities. South Asian immigrant women in North America, Britain, and Australia are often the targets of racial discrimination in addition to gender-based discrimination. Women of color often face disparities in access to healthcare and increased risks of maternal mortality. While many South Asian women may be upwardly mobile and belong to the so-called model minority, many of them face precarity in healthcare, economic stability, immigration status, and in domestic partnerships. This time of precarity that women are living in makes it all the more urgent to focus on women's lives, their creative expressions of trauma in poetry, not to wallow in their victimhood but chart paths towards renewed struggles for justice.

We have gathered the works of sixty-eight poets in this volume including ourselves, the editors. We are both scholars of postcolonial and American multicultural literatures, who grew up in India but are now located in US academia. We are also poets. Our volume represents poets from Bangladesh, India, Nepal, Pakistan, Sri Lanka and South Asian diasporas in the United Kingdom, United States, Canada, Australia and even Sweden. We believe our collection is substantive, but it is not exhaustive and does not represent all South Asian communities. We reached out to many poets through our networks by posting calls for poems on various websites and social media sites. We were not always able to get submissions from the poets we reached out to. So, our book should be considered only a first attempt at curating a volume on this topic and not a comprehensive collection of South Asian women's poetry. We hope future volumes in this area will feature poets we have not been able to include.

South Asian Poetry: Historical Origins

The geographic entity of South Asia includes the Indian subcontinent, Afghanistan, the island nations of Sri Lanka, the Maldives, and the Himalayan countries of Nepal and Bhutan. India, by its sheer size dominates this terrain. However, South Asia is a space of extraordinary diversity, even more so after colonization and migratory movements and formations of South Asian diaspora communities in the Caribbean Islands, Britain, North America and Australia. For centuries, India, before she was carved up into the countries that we have now, was the land of poetry. Poetry sprang from her breast, and she was born of the poetry of the ancient hymns, the Vedas, the myths and stories that were told orally, the prayers that were sung by men and women. Arundhati Subramaniam, a renowned contemporary South Asian poet, has recently edited a collection of ancient women's poetry from the Indian subcontinent titled *Wild Women: Seekers, Protagonists and Goddesses in Sacred Indian Poetry*. Not all examples of ancient women's poetry were lyrical or pastoral celebrations of love or Nature. Many told of the traumas of separation, even about Hindu goddesses like Durga and Kali, and the epic heroines such as Sita and Draupadi. *The Mahabharata*, an example of the quintessential myths of the land, tells of the patience and perseverance of women, of mothers, sisters, wives, and even warrior women. These stories re-emerge in contemporary rewritings of mythological women in our own collection. This is the tradition which we wish to honor as we and our poets tell of the traumas that make contemporary women sing, speak and weep in the poems collected here. Our anthology of poetry shows the strength and survival of South Asian women under traumatic conditions. This is not a collection of poems that solely focuses on the pain of trauma but is meant to show how women adapt to and prevail over trauma. So, while it seems as though our poets express pain, they also express a positive transformation. We offer these poems up to our readers as expressions of women's strength and endurance.

A whole literary critical system of aesthetics was embedded in the Vedas. *Kavya* or poetry and poetic form was just as important in the Indian literary tradition as it was in the Greek literary tradition. *Rasa* or essence "communicated sensibility" (Jussawalla 185), and *dhvani* or meaning, particularly as communicated through metaphors and descriptions of gestures, were essential to poetry, especially as poetry was the basis of drama. *Dhvani* or poetic verbal play, i.e., the poetic undertones to communicating experience, was and remains essential in the Indian literary tradition.

With the Delhi Sultanate and later the Mughals, came the Persian poetic forms of the long Persian epics, the stories of love lost and won, forms such as the *dastan*, (long lyrical poem) *ghazal* (couplets with an elaborate rhyme scheme), among others. Amir Khusrau (1253–1325 AD) is considered to be a pioneer of the *qawwali* and *ghazal* poetic forms, writing in an amalgam of Persian and Hindavi. Most importantly, he ushered in the tradition of Sufi poetry in India as a disciple of Nizamuddin Auliya. During the Mughal period, around 1562, Emperor Akbar commissioned the *Hamzanama*, an epic on the adventures of the Prophet Mohammed's uncle. Akbar was particularly interested in promoting poetry that drew from the Persian form of Firdausi's *Shahnama* (c. 1000). His reign inaugurated the great age of Muslim poetry in the subcontinent. Qawwali or poetic debate with didactic or proverbial endings dominated the Mughal court. The Mughals brought a special lyricality and poignancy which we see even today in contemporary Muslim poetry in English, often brought to us in translations from original languages.

In medieval and early modern South Asia, we witness the flourishing of the Sufi (starting in the 11th century) and Bhakti traditions (starting in the 8th century) which emphasized alternatives to Hindu or Islamic religious orthodoxy, stressing the importance of a personal relationship with the divine. Mirabai is one such female mystic from the early 1500s. Her devotional lyrics addressed to Lord Krishna as her lover are still sung today. This devotion to Krishna led to her social ostracism and worldly suffering but made her poetry immortal. Similarly, Lal Ded, the 14th-century Kashmiri mystic who, although Hindu, was recognized by Sufis as a saint, wrote poems which are still being disseminated through many English translations from the Kashmiri.

The eminent critic and first historian of Indian Literature in English, K.R. Srinivasa Iyengar, in his monumental *Indian Writing in English* (Asia Publishing House, 1963), wrote about the two sisters Aru and Toru Dutt, marking an important moment which hails the beginning, as it were, of Indian poetry in English. The sisters were educated in France and later moved to Cambridge, England where they studied and wrote poetry. When they returned to Calcutta, Aru succumbed to consumption. Toru poured her grief into a collection of poems, nostalgic for her time in France, entitled *A Sheaf Gleaned in French Fields*, in which she included eight poems by her late sister Aru. The book was well received, both in India and in Britain, where Edmund Gosse wrote: "When poetry is as good as this it does not matter whether Rouveyre prints it upon Whatman Paper or whether it steals to light in blurred type from some press in Bhowanipore" (Iyengar 57).

Bengal is the "motherland," as it were, of contemporary Indian Literature in English, as, in general, the literary and upper classes of Bengal were quick to embrace Western education. Even T.B. Macaulay in his 1835 Minute acknowledged that there were "natives who are quite competent to discuss political or scientific questions with fluency and precision in the English language," perhaps tangentially referring to Bengali intellectuals such as Raja Ram Mohan Roy. It is noteworthy that Rabindranath Tagore was the first Indian to win the Nobel Prize and drew the envious ire of W.B. Yeats: "… no Indian knows English. Nobody can write music and style in a language which is not their own" (Yeats 834–35). The persistence and pervasiveness of poetry in English by authors from South Asia, both in their land of origin and in the diaspora, underscores the importance of this genre for the development of literatures specific to the regions as also for what we now call "Postcolonial Literatures".

As is well known, South Asian poetry in English began in a colonialist mode. Often educated Indians under colonial rule willingly espoused colonial education as a means of modernization and as a means of getting their voices heard and for this reason, they often chose English as their medium of expression. They attempted to show the colonizer that they could do just as well, if not better, in the English language. Professor K. R. Srinivasa Iyengar writes that "they used [the English language] as the forceful means of communicating their meaning and message to India and the world" (Iyengar 15).

Our anthology consists predominantly of poets who write in English. However, it also includes poets who are bilingual, like Renu Gupta who has translated her poem from Hindi and Shamin Azad, a bilingual poet writing in Bengali and English. Additionally, Shelly Naz's poems in this collection have been translated by Kamrul Hassan. In an era of globalization and diasporic communities, it is unsurprising that poetry has become a fluid space moving between languages and national borders.

We must also acknowledge here the sometimes forgotten and often overlooked earlier critical perspectives on what we now call South Asian or Postcolonial Literatures. It is by tracing this literary history that we want to contextualize new work in the field. In the early 1990s, John Oliver Perry, a professor of English at Tufts University who took a keen interest in South Asian poetry in English, argued that studying contemporary "Indian English poetry should help in the general project to 'open up the canon' and liberate Americans from narrow critical views of what poetry or (literary culture) in English can be and thus, supposedly, must or should be" (Perry 2).

In a more recent essay on Indian literature in English, Vinay Dharwadker in a chapter titled "The Historical Formation of Indian English Literature" references the work of 19th-century poets like Henry Derozio, Michael Madhusudan Dutt and Toru Dutt, among others as being responsible for introducing Indian themes into English-language poetry. Dharwadker reads the poet Michael Madhusudan Dutt in particular as someone who "attempted to bend English usage. . . toward an imitation of syntax, imagery, and figuration of the Indian languages, particularly Bangla and Sanskrit" (Dharwadker 230), anticipating almost the hybrid aesthetics of Salman Rushdie. After mapping major currents in 19th- and 20th-century literature, Dharwadker ends with a discussion of cosmopolitanism and the rise of diaspora writers who finally manage to make English resemble Indian languages. However, even though he mentions some poets like Meena Alexander and Sujata Bhatt, Dharwadker focuses more on contemporary novelists rather than poets of today.

It is important, at this point, to talk about the influence of Sarojini Naidu (1879–1949), the distinguished activist in the Indian Independence movement who was honoured with the title of "Nightingale of India" for her poetry by Mahatma Gandhi. Her poetry was widely taught in schools in the immediate post-independence period. "The Bangle Sellers" is a poem by Naidu that was widely anthologized and recited by Indian schoolchildren in the last century:

> Bangle sellers are we who bear
> Our shining loads to the temple fair...
> Who will buy these delicate, bright
> Rainbow-tinted circles of light?

Also important was her poem titled "The Queen's Rival", a moving verse about the love of parents for their child. The poem imagines a conversation between Queen Gulnaar and King Feroz, where she asks the king to bring her a rival; responding to the challenge, he brings her their daughter.

Critics who believe that Sarojini Naidu created exotica fail to contextualize her and locate her in the high Persian literary traditions of Hyderabad and their hybrid interplay with Western colonial influences. While it can be said that she echoed her Western education, especially that of the Romantic poets, it must also be added that her poetry was particularly located in the physical contexts of Hyderabad and Secunderabad, and reflected a mix of the literary, aristocratic Mughal diction and the more colloquial language of the cantonments.

While Sarojini Naidu is best known for lyrical poetry, we must remember what India's first Prime Minister Nehru most recognized her for. Nehru wrote:

> She began life as a poetess. In later years,
> when the compulsion of events drew her
> into the national struggle and she threw
> herself into it with all the zest and fire she
> possessed, she did not write poetry with
> pen and paper but her whole life became a
> poem and a song.
>
> — (Nehru Qtd in Iyengar 222)

Additionally, Naidu's verses paint vibrant images of Indian mythology and rural life, often not familiar to non-Indian audiences at the time, and laid the foundation for many women to feel the courage to express themselves, not only in English but in their mother tongues and to use the language to speak out against both societal and colonialist norms.

In 1969, P. Lal published his *Modern Indian Poetry in English: An Anthology and a Credo*, attempting to collect and locate poetry written in the subcontinent. He also established the Writers' Workshop and press, which brought to the fore several Indian poets who had been writing separately in various journals. Through this endeavor, several male poets emerged, such as Dom Moraes, Nissim Ezekiel, A.K. Ramanujan, Keki Daruwalla, R. Parthasarathy, and most prominently and continuing to compose even now, Adil Jussawalla. With R. Parthasarathy's poem "The Iron of English Rings on my Tongue", the whole issue of the suitability of English as a poetic medium for Indians whose understanding of English prosody may be inexact and yet whose intentions may be to convey through English an Indian sensibility was reopened. Most of the introductions written to a whole series of both anthologies of poetry and anthologies of criticisms of Indian poetry in English seem to dwell on the issue of whether the English language should continue to be a medium of expression. But as we can see today from the great success and recognition of diaspora poets writing in English such as Imtiaz Dharker, Sujata Bhatt, the late Meena Alexander, Suniti Namjoshi, among others, the question of whether South Asians should write in English or not, is moot, as English writers, whether writing poetry or fiction, have shown themselves to be distinguished in the general landscape of South Asian literature.

Indeed, the hybridization of English to express an anti-colonial attitude is the hallmark of postcolonial writing. The major exponent of this capturing of Indian English in poetry was Nissim Ezekiel (1952–2004), whose poem "Goodbye Party for Miss Pushpa T.S." (Ezekiel 190) led to much controversy, because it seemed that it was written in what was then considered "Poor English". Several critics and poets such as Dom Moraes and U.R. Ananthamurthy criticized such experiments as Ezekiel's "Very Indian Poem in Indian English" (Ezekiel 268), meant to be a parody, as an inability to write in "good" English (Jussawalla 55–63). Critics such as Linda Hess bemoaned Indian English linguistic experimentation (Hess 40) for instance, in her chapter, "The Problem of Style," in *The Twice-Born Fiction* (1971). Meenakshi Mukherjee, one of the earliest foremothers of Indian English literary criticism, addressed the issue of Indians writing in English as one faced by a people who do not normally speak or think in English and, consequently, "...each writer has to forge the medium that will best answer his needs (Mukherjee172–173)." However:

> A critic of the Indian poet in English must
> see these poets at their point in the multi-
> cultural, multilingual situation and proceed
> out of an awareness of this situation so that
> an overemphasis on the stylistic problems
> or simply on thought does not overbear the
> work of the poem. (Jussawalla 62).

Emerging out of this discussion and discourse of whether to write in English or not was an extremely controversial literary figure, Kamala Das. She broke forth with her credo "I write poetry in English because I have found writing in English a little less difficult than writing in Malayalam" and "The language one employs is not important. What is important is the thought contained in the words" (Das qtd in P. Lal 102).

It is interesting to note that an Indian sense of lyricality also pervades Kamala Das's most daring poem, "The Dance of the Eunuchs":

> It was hot, so hot, before the eunuchs came
> To dance, wide skirts going round and round,
>
> Cymbals...

The echoing alliterations, the capturing of the rhythm of the dance and the shock of unlikely analogies and allegories, such as "funeral pyres" and "urine of lizards and mice" create an antecedent for poems appearing in our own volume, because they echo the voices of the marginalized, the "outcasted," and those of alternate sexualities. Das's life covered many twists and turns (and conversions), opening the way for queer Indian writers such as Hoshang Merchant, Devdutt Pattanaik, Vijayarajamallika, Suniti Namjoshi. Her two collections of poetry *My Story* and *Alphabet of Lust* broke forth with then-taboo subjects. Usha Akella's poem "Porcupine", in this collection pays tribute to Kamala Das's "My Story".

A legendary poet and critic herself, Eunice De Souza lauded Kamala Das for her openness about autobiographical experiences and her "genuine core of pain" (De Souza in *Indian Poetry in English* 19). De Souza likens Das to the American confessional poets, Sylvia Plath and Anne Sexton, and writes, "It is this confrontation with pain, pain in relation to sex and the family—both fundamental archetypal experiences—that gives readers it seems to me, a point of contact with these intensely subjective poems and enables them to be moved by them, sometimes profoundly" (De Souza in *Indian Poetry in English* 21). With her verses, Kamala Das opened the road for several of the poets in this collection, who write of their pain and suffering in family situations, societal rejections, and political persecutions. This is what transforms into the "traumas" expressed by the poets in our volume today.

The pioneering work of Toru Dutt, Sarojini Naidu, and Kamala Das thus paved the way for women poets like Meena Alexander, Imtiaz Dharker, and Suniti Namjoshi in the late 20th and 21st centuries. It is important to note that here we witness a transition from South Asian nations to diasporic communities. Alexander's contributions span many genres, but she is most remembered for her lyrical memoir *Fault Lines* as well as many volumes of poetry. In her work, Alexander grapples with many censored aspects of women's experiences, including childhood sexual molestation, birth, and postpartum depression.

Sujata Bhatt and Imtiaz Dharker are two other diasporic poets of the same generation as Alexander. Both are based in Europe, Dharker in Scotland, and Bhatt in Germany. Bhatt continues the path of foregrounding women's bodily experiences in her poetry, including their unabashed desire for erotic pleasure (Basu, 2016, 393–94). She said in an interview "I always felt that I should be able to write about whatever concerned me without being censored. I've always felt the need to break certain silences and yes to bear witness" (Tookey 32–34). This focus on eroticism is interspersed in her poetry with the layered memories of the places she encounters in Germany and their echoes of the historical trauma of the Holocaust.

Imtiaz Dharker is a Pakistani-born poet who lives and works in Scotland. She was considered for the position of Poet Laureate of Britain in 2019, which she declined in order to concentrate on her creative rather than public-facing work. In her early volumes like *Purdah*, Dharker's poetry is critical of practices in Muslim societies that limit the lives and freedoms of women. In her later volumes like *The Terrorist at My Table,* Dharker responds in her poems to the injustices unleashed on Muslims as a result of the global War on Terror and its mechanisms of surveillance (Basu, 2016, 399). These poems affirm her solidarity with fellow Muslims, even though she had been vocal in the past about many Islamic institutions entrenched in patriarchy.

Suniti Namjoshi is another woman poet born in the mid-twentieth century who has lived in India, US, and Canada and now resides in England. She has been a prolific poet and fabulist, publishing ten volumes of poetry. Her poetry and prose collections challenge racism and patriarchy from her unique perspective of a South Asian lesbian feminist. Namjoshi's collection of fabulist tales *The Mothers of Maya Diip*, envisions a feminist utopia in the tradition of Rokeya Sekhawat Hossain's *Sultana's Dream* (1905) in which the protagonist dreams of a land where women govern and men serve. However, Namjoshi's greater achievement lies perhaps in her collection of poems *Snapshots of Caliban*, discussed extensively by Harveen S. Mann. Mann argues that Namjoshi "defies the practice of male, postcolonialist, dialectical appropriations of Caliban as colonized- and- resistant man by recasting Shakespeare's character as a Third World lesbian subject" (Mann 100). Namjoshi's other poems express her sense of alienation within dominant discourses of religion, nationalism, and patriarchy. This sense of exile parallels the mood in Agha Shahid Ali's poetry. Agha Shahid Ali was a Kashmiri American poet whose achievement was unfortunately short-lived due to his untimely death from brain cancer in 2001. He was a gay, Muslim poet from Kashmir whose "themes of exile, loss, nostalgia, and his political concerns are expressed largely through an engagement with history and memory" (Ahmad 376). He was the subject of a major collection of essays *The World of Agha Shahid Ali*, which was edited by Tapan Kumar Ghosh & Sisir Kumar Chatterjee and published by SUNY in 2021. Even though Agha Shahid Ali did not deal directly with homoeroticism in his poetry, his formal innovation, especially his perfecting of the ghazal in English, inspired many poets to experiment with this form and other queer Muslim poets like Kazim Ali to chart new paths in poetry.

Among South Asian women poets who have had a formative influence in the development of this literary genre, we would like to mention Jean Arasanayagam. Arasanayagam (1931–2019) who was of Dutch Burgher ancestry, thus occupying a unique place in postcolonial Sri Lanka, as she embodied both Dutch colonial and Sri Lankan postcolonial heritage. Moreover, although she did not belong to the two groups, Sinhala or Tamil, involved in the long Sri Lankan Civil War, her marriage to a Jaffna Tamil activist made her the target of attack in the infamous Black July pogroms against Tamil communities in Sri Lanka in 1983. She experienced these events first hand as her family was threatened with violence and eventually had to move to a refugee camp while they were living in Kandy and she was working in Peradeniya College.

These experiences found expression in her collection of poems *Apocalypse 83*, which is a remarkable document of an internal refugee at the beginning of the Sri Lankan Civil War. However, more than a testimony of atrocity, it is deeply introspective, examining her own identity and vocation as a poet in the midst of this crisis. The critic Shelby E. Ward argues that these acts of witnessing violence become "the very acts that can allow for and open a space and a dialogue for forgiveness and possibly even reconciliation" (Ward 55). In the concluding lines of the poem "Innocent victim-Trincomalee," Arasanyagam writes:

> My house went up in flames
> Together with
> My sister. father. mother.
> And will they come again?
> Strangers? (Apocalypse 83, 30)

Ward points out that the perpetrators of ethnic violence are called strangers, "they have no ethnic or political markers" (Ward 57). In post-conflict Sri Lanka, these poems from four decades ago still provide a path forward towards reconciliation

In our condensed overview of South Asian poetry in English, we have only highlighted women poets whom we consider pioneers in the field. As with any anthology or introduction, we are aware that there are omissions in our survey. We are not attempting to recognize the major poets of each decade of the 20th and 21st centuries. The poets featured in our volume are those who are living and who have been active mostly in the last two decades. There are too many poets who are still active who have been productive prior to the poets featured in this volume, whose work and impact we have not been able to discuss. Our focus has been to offer a selection of women's poets from a variety of countries in South Asia who respond to trauma in poetic form. This volume, we hope, will inspire readers to trace other poets working today on trauma and those who have worked on it in the past and thus bring the poems in this volume into a productive dialog with others.

REFERENCES

Ahmad, Hena. "First and Foremost . . . A Poet in the English Language": Agha Shahid Ali" A *History of Indian Poetry in English,* edited by Rosinka Chowdhury. Cambridge University Press, 2016, pp. 375–388.

Alexander, Meena. *Fault Lines.* The Feminist Press at CUNY, 2020.

Anand, Mulk Raj and Eleanor Zelliot, editors. *An Anthology of Dalit Literature.* South Asia Books, 1992.

Arasanayagam, Jean. *Apocalypse 83.* International Center for Ethnic Studies, 2003.

Amirthanayagm, Guy, editor. *Writers in East West Encounter: New Cultural Bearings.* London: Macmillan, 1982.

Ansari, Ameena Kazi and Anisur Rahman, editors. *Indian English Women Poets.* India, Creative Books, 2009.

Baldwin, Shauna Singh. *What the Body Remembers.* Anchor, 1999.

Basu, Lopamudra. "The Languages of Diaspora: Meena Alexander, Sujata Bhatt, Imtiaz Dharker." edited by Rosinka Chaudhuri in *A History of Indian Poetry in English.* United States, Cambridge UP, 2016, pp. 389–403.

—. "Rohingya Refugee Poetry: Testimony and Cultural Activism"in *Narratives of Trauma in South Asian Literature,* edited *by* Gautam Karmakar and Zeenat Khan. Routledge, 2023. pp. 260–271.

Basu Lopamudra and Cynthia Leenerts, editors. *Passage to Manhattan: Critical Essays on Meena Alexander.* Cambridge Scholars Publishing, 2009.

Bhatt, Sujata. *Collected Poems.* Carcanet Press, 2013.

Bond, Lucy and Stef Craps. *Trauma (The New Critical Idiom).* Routledge, 2020.

Butalia, Urvashi. *The Other Side of Silence: Voices from the Partition of India.* Durham: Duke UP, 2000

Byrne, James and Shehzar Doja, editors. *I am Rohingya: Poetry from the Camps and Beyond.* Arc Publications, 2019.

Chaudhuri, Rosinka, editor. *A History of Indian Poetry in English*. United States, Cambridge UP, 2016.

Chirantan, Kulshrestha, editor. *Contemporary Indian English Verse: An Evaluation*. Delhi: Arnold Heinemann, 1980.

Craps, Stef. "Beyond Eurocentrism: Trauma Theory in the Global Age." *The Future of Trauma*

Theory: Contemporary Literary and Cultural Criticism. edited by Gert Buelens, Sam Durrant and Robert Eaglestone. New York: Routledge, 2014. pp 45–61.

Dharker, Imtiaz. *Purdah and Other Poems*. Oxford UP, 1988.

—. *The Terrorist at My Table*. Bloodaxe, 2006,

Dharwadker, Vinay. "The Historical Formation of Indian-English Literature" in *Literary Cultures in History: Reconstructions from South Asia*, edited by Sheldon Pollock. University of California Press, 2003, pp. 199–267.

Daruwalla, Keki, editor. *Two Decades of Indian Poetry 1960-1980*. New Delhi: Vicass Publishing House, 1980.

Das, Kamala. *Alphabet of Lust*. Orient Black Swan, 1976.

—. "The Dance of the Eunuchs." *Summer in Calcutta*, Everett Press, 1965. https://www.poemhunter.com/poem/the-dance-of-the-eunuchs/.

—. *My Story*. Sterling Publishers,1976 https://archive.org/stream/in.ernet.dli.2015.220167/2015.220167.My-Story_djvu.txt

De Souza, Eunice, "Kamala Das" in Indian Poetry in English: Essays in Criticism edited by Shahane, V.A. and M. Sivaramkrishna. Hyderabad: Osmania UP, 1977. pp.19–27.

—. editor. *Nine Indian Women Poets: An Anthology*. Oxford UP, 1998.

Doniger, Wendy. *The Hindus: An Alternative History*. Penguin, 2010.

Dutt, Toru. *A Sheaf Gleaned in French Fields*. Saptahik Sambad Press, 1876. https://books.google.com.cy/books?id=5MgFAAAAQAA-J&printsec=frontcover#v=onepage&q&f=false

Ezekiel, Nissim. *Collected Poems*. Second Edition. Preface by Leela Gandhi Oxford University Press, 1989.

Ghosh, Tapan Kumar and Sisir Kumar Chatterjee, editors. *The World of Agha Shahid Ali*. SUNY Press, 2021.

Gilroy, Paul. *There Ain't No Black in the Union Jack*. Routledge, 1987.

Hess, Linda. "Post-Independence Indian Poetry in English." *Considerations*, edited by Meenakshi Mukherjee. Arnold Heinemann, 1977. 38–40.

Hossain, Rokeya. *Sultana's Dream and Padmarg*. Translated by Barnita Bagchi. Penguin, 2022.

Iyengar, Srinivasa K.R. *Indian Writing in English*. Asia Publishing House, 2nd edition, 1973.

Jussawalla, Feroza. *Family Quarrels: Towards a Criticism of Indian Writing in English*. Peter Lang, 1984.

Karmakar, Goutam and Zeenat Khan, editors. *Narratives of Trauma in South Asian Literature*. Routledge, 2022.

King, Bruce. *Modern Indian Poetry in English*. Oxford UP, 1987.

Lal, P. *Modern Indian Poetry in English: An Anthology and a Credo*. Writers Workshop, 1969.

Macaulay, T.B. "Macaulay's Minute on Indian Education 2nd, February, 1835." Part of the History of English Studies Page, UC Santa Barbara, uploaded 1995.

Mann, Harveen S. "Suniti Namjoshi: Diasporic, Lesbian Feminism and the Textual Politics of Transnationality." *The Journal of the Midwest Modern Language Association*. vol 30, no 1–2, 1997. pp. 97-113.

Menon, Ritu and Kamla Bhasin. *Borders and Boundaries: Women in India's Partition*. Rutgers U P, 1998.

Mukherjee, Meenakshi. *The Twice-Born Fiction*. Arnold-Heinemann 1971.

Naidu, Sarojini. "Bangle-sellers" *The Bird of Time: Songs of Life, Death, and the Spring*. New York: John Lane, London: William Heinemann, 1912. pp 64–65 https://www.rarebooksocietyofindia.org/book_archive/196174216674_10151_49982251675.pdf

—. "The Queen's Rival" *The Golden Threshold*. London 1896. https://www.gutenberg.org/cache/epub/680/pg680-images.html

Namjoshi, Suniti. *The Blue Donkey Fables and The Mothers of Maya Diip*. Penguin, 1991.

Nayar, Pramod. "Trauma, Testimony, and Human Rights: Women's Atrocity Narratives from Postcolonial India." In *Perspectives on South Asian Women's Writing*, edited by Feroza Jussawalla and Deborah Weagel, *South Asian Review*, vol 29, no 1, 2008, pp. 27–44.

Parthasarathy, R. ed. *Ten 20th-Century Indian Poets in English*. Delhi: Oxford UP, 1976.

Peeradina, Saleem. *Contemporary Indian Poetry in English*. Bombay: Macmillan, 1972.

Perry, John Oliver. 1993. "The Cultural Situation Of Indian English Poetry And Its Criticism Today." *South Asian Review*, vol. 17, no. 14, pp. 1–17, doi:10.1080/02759527.1993.11932155.

Pollock, Sheldon. Introduction. *Literary Cultures in History: Reconstructions from South Asia*, edited by. Sheldon Pollock. University of California Press, 2003, pp. 1–36.

Pritish, Nandy, editor. *Indian Poetry in English Today*. New Delhi: Sterling, 1973.

Ramazani, Jahan. *The Hybrid Muse: Postcolonial Poetry in English*. University of Chicago Press, 2001.

Rowland, Anthony. *Poetry as Testimony: Witnessing and Memory in Twentieth Century Poems*. Routledge, 2014.

Sidhwa, Bapsi. *Cracking India*. Minneapolis: Milkweed, 1991.

Spivak, Gayatri Chakravorty. "Can the Subaltern Speak?" *Colonial Discourse and Postcolonial Theory: A Reader*, edited by Patrick Williams and Laura Chrisman, Columbia University Press, 1999, pp. 66–111.

Subramaniam, Arundhati, editor. *Wild Women: Seekers, Protagonists and Goddesses in Sacred Indian Poetry*. Penguin India, 2024.

Shahane, V.A. and M. Sivaramkrishna. *Indian Poetry in English: Essays in Criticism*. Hyderabad: Osmania UP, 1977.

Singh, Amrijit, Rajiva Verma, and Irene Joshi. *Indian Literature in English 1827–1979: A Guide to Information Sources*. Gale's Research, Detroit, 1982.

Tookey, Helen. "In Conversation with Sujata Bhatt" *PN Review*, vol. 40, no. 1, 2013, pp. 30–32.

Ward, Shelby E. "My Body was a Poem: Jean Arasanayagam's Poetic Body as Witness and Judge in Sri Lanka's Ethnic Conflict." *Kairos: A Journal of Critical Symposium*, vol. 2, no.1, 2017, pp. 51–66.

Yeats, William Butler. *The Letters of W.B Yeats*. Edited by Allan Wade. Rupert Hart-Davis, 1954

VINITA AGRAWAL

YASHODHARA[1]

The upturned bowl of the night sky glittering with stars
and your man walking out of your life, Yashodhara

Pay attention to the silence
silence is the most wilful mauler

the yellow fault of his robes
Down, down, down into the darkness

Your bitter bed, cradling your gentle son
dried garnet drops bleeding from wounded fissures in tree barks

Clouds, winds, leaves, flowers have all lost speech
Light has washed colour out, to the brown resin of mummies

Such stillness Yashodhara as though nothing will ever move again
such grating vacuum, it could stifle enlightenment's voice

He will come back but only to take away your ten-year-old son
His begging bowl his legacy to his child

He will bequeath it to its rightful inheritor
and walk away again, eastward, second time around.

The upturned bowl of the night sky
will appear bereft of every star that ever was

JA

Ja in Sanskrit means born from -
ambuja, neerja, pankaja, saroja
Born from water.
Synonyms for lotus.
The flower that grows in mud, unstained
like the sun rising from night.

You were a lotus in my womb.
cradled in the waters of birth.
I held on to you with my breaths.
Every inhalation
filling your pink lungs with life
for you to emerge unstained.

But they wouldn't let you.
They, who wanted more sperms
in the family, than ovaries.
They stained your immaculate body
with knives.

I've bled so much since then
that when I walk
red liquid seeps from my feet.
Like the Buddha,
I leave lotus marks
with every step I take
ambuja, neerja, pankaja, saroja.*

'Ja' was previously published in Drunken Boat *Issue#25*

ZAITHOON BIN AHAMED

A TWIST OF FREEDOM

The odor of smoke still lingers in the backyard of the simple,
mud-hut home
As she picks up the pieces, literally, of what's left behind
It baffles her as to how and why a senseless act of carnage
could be heart-wrenching, but also in some way relieving

The promise of happily ever after ended just less than a year
of marital bliss
When Kani announced to her family-in-law of her inability to bear
There were moments of hope, but they were soon washed
away in a gush of blood
Followed by abusive words and blows to the stomach of this
'non-worthy bitch'

Efforts to escape were thwarted in time
Within the confines of a black, soot kitchen, Kani lived her life
in pitiful sorrow
Sometimes like an imbecile, embracing anything that resembles
a foetus close to her heart
He had stopped trying, she had lost feeling

He was a convict, on the run
Having run away from the freedom fighters of his
ancestral colony
His struggle was different and complex
The wounds and scars still fresh from the last onslaught, he
made his escape
Only to be trapped in another battle of unworthiness for not
producing a successor

Torn between two worlds, his only source of love and frustration was Kani

The fateful day arrived
Three rugged men rushed in and Kani stood in the doorway in an apparent effort to mislead
This time she gave in and switched sides
With a blink of an eye, she showed them the way through the hut
There was a startled scream followed by seven deafening shots
He fell to the ground in a pool of blood as the red-dirt swirled around his motionless body

The men went away
There were no tears as she dragged his blood-soaked body into the shade
And prepared to wail in pretence sorrow for the public eye
A train of sympathizers formed quickly
But for Kani, it was the beginning of a new life of freedom

USHA AKELLA

PORCUPINE

> Illness has become my mate, bound by ties of blood and nerves and bone,
> and I hold with it long secret conversations.
>
> —Kamala Das, *My Story* (p. 212)

Where does she hide,

    the one who sends black meteors in the canvas of my skin?

I was born a girl I suppose, I've now become a porcupine,

all that touches me pricks, all that I touch is pricked.

Burning effigy in a desert I don't stop burning.

Iceberg. I am frozen. I don't thaw.

I digest nothing   I roam black tunnels at night,

I am a dart board   unskinned animal salted,

    dervish-vertigo prays often in my head.

And other such creatures:

aposematic tiger moth   cuttlefish   p i t o h u i s :
    what I ingest, I emit,

I grow quills, I am toxic, my skin is prickled leaves,

blue-ringed   blue-throated   blue-bruise planet,

I become yellow when approached,

Crown-of-thorn starfish in royal purple my spines are sharp.

I am an ecosystem of pain.

Neck turning on creaking hinges,

muscle-fibers are wood,

diaphanous jellyfish   I sting myself   a glance can tear my skin.

As a knife scr a p in g bread a n d crum b l i n g,
I am the knife, the bread and the crumbling crumbs,

not veins but rope,

not skin but shroud,

my days are a sunset to sunset,

fibro m y a l g i a
thoughts sizzle apart like weak batter on a pan.

Will I ever emerge through a wormhole

crowned with stars?*

'Porcupine' was previously published in I Will Not Bear You Sons *by Usha Akella (Spinifex Press, 2021).*

NAMING

for Jyoti, Delhi rape survivor

We want the world to know her real name. My daughter didn't do anything
wrong, she died while protecting herself. I am proud of her. Revealing her
name will give courage to other women who have survived these attacks.
They will find strength from my daughter.

—Father of Jyoti,[1] Delhi rape case, 2012 BBC Hindi.

She was returning home from watching *Life of Pi,*
the hero lived to tell the tale
in a boat shared with animals ... was this a sign from
fate? Her journey in a bus with predators:

                    six men falling
                         upon her like hyenas,
             a wheel jack handle and metal rod plunged
in her private parts, the intestines ripped out,
in a moving bus circumambulating Munirka,
bite marks across her body ... death in a Singapore hospital.

Her mother's eyes were dark charcoal, unspilled lakes,
She died but we die every day ... Kudrat bhi ne hamara saath nahin diya[2]

        When the dots finally connected they were black,
black gags, gnashes across their mouths, black dressed,
the women gathered in India Gate, Raisina Hill,
the drum beat of marching feet in cities spelt *Justice* ...

               women as petroleum, she the wick
                keeping the flame burning.
If this day is a fruit, it is a papaya, with a black heart
in the gaudy gold of a nation; if a flower, the frangipani,
its milky sap blistering a nation's veins; if a fish, *vaam,*

---

[1] By Indian law a rape victim's name is not published. The victim was given the
    name Nirbhaya in the media.

[2] *Kudrat bhi ne hamara saath nahin diya.:* Even God was not on our side.

as her intestines like eels on the bus floor;
if a tree, the tamarind souring the breath of India.

And if a name: Jyoti
emerginig like a lion from a cave,
whisking the world like a tornado,
Enough! *

* *'Naming' was previously published in* I Will Not Bear You Sons *by Usha Akella (Spinifex Press, 2021).*

DILRUBA Z. ARA

INHERITANCE OF PAIN

Within the womb, we inherit
Seeds of classification, sown deep,
Bound by societal norms and tradition,
A predetermined script we're to keep.

Boys, permanent fixtures in their kin,
Their roots intertwined, steadfast and sure,
While girls, transient guests within,
Bound to leave, their worth unsure.

Years gone, I left my childhood home,
Only to become a guest, a fleeting shadow,
In my in-laws' halls, I've roamed,
An outsider, longing for a place to be bestowed.

With every step, I carry the weight
Of generations past, their pain my cloak,
Their silenced voices, their unspoken fate,
Echoing within, a legacy bespoke.

My identity, fragmented and lost,
In the labyrinth of expectations, I roam,
Each breath a reminder of the cost,
Of burying dreams, of making a home.

And as I contemplate my own seed,
The burden of inheritance weighs heavy,
I wonder, will my children be freed
From the trauma passed down, relentless and unsteady?

For the cycle continues, unbroken,
Trauma given from mother to child,
Inheritors of pain, words left unspoken,
In the silence, our voices, defiled.

But hope flickers, a fragile flame,
In the darkness, a beacon of light,
Perhaps one day, we'll break the chain,
And rewrite the story, reclaim our right.

LEGACY

In the waning light of mother's halo,
Her eyes widen, senses sharpen.
Her heart is under a knife,
A stone under her tongue.
mind styled to be estranged.
Mama's eyes—sinister landscape.
Papa looks away.

The navel string,
Tightens around her neck,
Walks her. Back and forth!
A game of denial and protection.
Moments of innocence—slaughtered fast.
Warm in mother's hand,
A chunk of her heart drips blood.

Mama rolls it into a ball
For her sons to kick it around.
The girl chases—love, life,
The slice of her heart.
in mama's eyes,
baby snakes dance,
the boys, her future custodians.

Dusk falls,
Mamma catches the heart-ball;
Chops it up.
Gives her sons a part apiece,
Papa nods.
Centuries departed revisited;
A girl's heart is worth
half as much of her brothers'.

Stage set. Roles imposed.
The girl runs in circles,
Childhood twisted.

Through this darkness,
Massacre of trust,
Memories compete to be chosen,
To keep her alive—fool herself,
For decades.

Mama & papa now
Two crooked shadows,
Daughters-in-law, their keepers.
Sons, with laughter of a jackal,
Lick the blood that drips
From their sister's heart,
Make them fatter,
Hiding behind a religious façade,
Parade in family charades,
Where even God fears to interfere.

SHAMIM AZAD

ADD-ONS

Everyone is at the risk of discrimination,
financial loss or destitution.
Things are getting worse.
People are worried about all sort of displacements.
Even a coward and a skinny man
suddenly can make a strong attack on you!
Anyone and everyone can be
apprehensive of conflict and war,
fear for dying of thirst and hunger
wherever you are.
The loss of wealth, suffering of separation
is normal in this unfair world.

But if you are a woman,
you have inevitable trauma
for your personal insecurity
simply because of your body.

PARDON ME

People say forgiveness is a divine virtue.
It puts you in a higher place than
the criminal, the sinner.
Lenity will make you move on
The density of the dark memory
can fade away and will become thinner.

But just the thought of the matter
to consider
before even making an effort
my horrific memory appears like a fresh wound.
My fear feels like fire.
I see those breathless stairs,
smell the horrific odor,
hear the unbearable sound,
I feel the rapists' faces are just over there!
Fifty year old liberation struggle
becomes alive, vivid and clear.
Which is why
I choose not to pardon them ever.

KANWALPREET BAIDWAN

THE TRAVAILS IN THE BEDROOM

My bedroom is also my dungeon

Of humiliation, of extreme disrespect,

For my body and soul,

And to my very existence.

It saps away my strength,

And renders me lifeless,

Every moment, every night,

The foozled love-making,

Suffocating and claustrophobic,

Very different from my imagination,

 For I grew up visualising dreams,

Of the sensitive, caring male,

Of the Mills and Boons,

Alive and existing in stories galore.

But how do I comprehend and digest,

The raw, ruthless appetite,

Of the ravaging Indian patriarchal man,

Who merely satiates his lust,

Using my body only

To create his progeny?

I hate being starved,

Unfulfilled and unexplored.

So, I resist this inhumane silent torture

By applauding those women

Who move around uninhibited,

Taking pride in their sexuality,

At ease with their body,

And its very needs and identity.

I laud their efforts,

To be heard, cared,

And to be cherished.

I applaud their voice,

Airing their bodily hunger.

Indian women have felt

Embarrassed too long

Of their bodily needs,

The time has dawned,

When women are heralding in change,

In that very vicious den

Often called the 'master bedroom'

Where the woman is not just a figure,

But an equal partner,

Sometimes even the owner,

Of not only the bedroom

But also of her existence,

And of her own

Beautiful, gorgeous body.

PRAGYA BAJPAI

HIDDEN EYES

No one knows about my hidden eyes and nose
Naked eyes are easily beguiled by the visuals
Five senses were not enough to protect me
I planted more to safeguard my living-dead body
from the consequence of hurting
the male ego with bold defiance
I swear I can't be maimed again

Strange hands slipping inside me
have opened a third eye
Now, I read between the lines, I see with my mind
I know the difference between a gaze, stare, look and see
Understanding the language of eyes is no big deal
It has haunted me ever since I was five

I hear the footsteps of brutes in daylight too
Holding chocolates in one hand and a finger to the lips
Makes me sick. I am now allergic
to chocolates and the cough syrup too smells of them

It drugs my subconscious and makes me breathless
Chokes my throat, suffocates me to death
How can I forget that mercilessness
that bitter taste of his sweat smeared neck
He didn't kill me
but spared my life to die each day.

ALKA BALAIN

SHE ROSE TO HER REQUIREMENT *

A sunflower to the Sun,
I put aside my aspirations.
Suppressing my desires,
I am miserable. To find joy
in a well-kept house is not me.

I lose myself to fit in his life.
Trailing spouse, I want not to be.
Deep buried sleep my dreams:
I learned to call his mine.

It lay unmentioned—as the Sea
Develop Pearl, and Weed,
But only to ~~Himself~~ Herself—be known
The Fathoms they abide —

Supermoon in Singapore sky,
the moon in fullness in borrowed light.
Emily's book and I in a periapsis.
Mona Lisa from the Louvre bookmarks,
She rose to His Requirement – dropt.
I virgule His and write Her.

LAKSMISREE BANERJEE

THE DESECRATED MOTHER *

that night the shimmering stars
hid themselves in utter shame
as did the night while watching
the monstrosity of the dark game—

the bleary-eyed Mother wept and wept
with tears of endless riverine blood,
are these the goons I gave birth to
soaked in such a pernicious flood?
they walked in with hate and lust
wrapped in mantles of murk and evil
they besmeared the motherly bond holy
with claws and paws like the devil—

they throttled, raped and ripped her apart
with inhuman torture in caverns of stress
as darkness wished to hide in the dark
to run away from being such a witness—

intoxicated with blind Dionysian fury
they forgot their mother in their black souls
they forgot the warmth of her lap and milk
as they defiled brutally their Genesis whole—

* *In painful memory of a Global Protest/ Social Revolution against the Brutal Rape*
& Murder of a Female Doctor in RG Kar Hospital, Kolkata, India on 9th August-
---Focus on the Universal Movement of Justice for Women Reclaiming their
Rightful Space across Societies & Communities, 2024

yet who was she among many wounded like us?
Was she a Draupadi or an innocent Ahalya
was she a Lucrece or an unfortunate Leda,
or one among us reared with love's nectar?
or was she the Crusader full of Truth' s ambrosia?
Now she is both a living death and deadly life
A volcano, a conflagration, unstoppable fighter
she is now ready to erupt with dire fire
To avenge and heal with the Mother's ire—

She is now our ignited Womanhood, an invincible Abhaya!

I GROW IN DEATH

you split my tongue
you slit my throat
you slash my wings
you cut my clitoris
you hack my foliage—

my silence is your delusion
my voicelessness
embers of my soul in rage
my body a cemetery
of speaking ashes in full bloom
you smell the purgatorial ambrosia
of my incensed fragrance—

from Egypt to Congo
from Amazon to India
my trails of travails make me
green, red and pure gold
smitten with wan flames
I revel in my firewood-pain
a ruptured spirit ever unfurling
my throat cut resonates endlessly
a croaking frog dancing in the rain—

my split tongue now
breeds poison
the serpent of your creation
perhaps a snapdragon ready
with your mesh of deceit
a rose re-incarnated as cactus
spiky, unforgiving, sculpted
through tyranny—

as you cut so I grow
more you suck more I flow
my life eternal brazen in death
as my skeletal branches flail
they splice you
lacerate you—

I rise in my new vision
you fall in your remorseless delusion
my living death now my azure
the bird of love
a snake in the sky—

THIRST

the brown wilted leaves dusky in whorls
cuddled in parched mud
can hardly breathe
some of them still hang
on twigs of the crooked tree
with a bent broken spine
unquenched forever
along the thirsty salt-laden shores
of an orange-grey sundown—

the withered flowers gasping on ground
trapeze in a dance of death
fiercely rolling in a wayward breeze
stuffed heartlessness invites
the dark clandestine night—

I sit lonely with the warrior waves
thrashing my feet frail
with endless walking
in search of sea shells with live molluscs
hoping to find an oyster
with a brilliant pearl to hide in me
a shelter from the tradesmen out there—

I wait for the drowsy sun
to drop into my lap lovingly
for a tranquil sleep—

yet nothingness is all
no scintillating pearl
no warm love in sight
as the sun dives into
the abysmal cold waters
leaving behind the fathomless night
myself lost in an eternity
of search
for the light!

SCARS

No, my scars could never
melt into the blue, they seethed
they breathed till

They have come to blossom
as strength stronger
than truth

As beauty more beautiful
than flowers, as fire more
radiant than bridal lava

As armour more formidable
than death—

I shall remember the way
you took your way out
into a new future

Discarding me like
a burnt log or some sterile
dirt of the desert

Or a brittle parchment
not worth the deciphering
Or some dried up rose
smothered in cinders—

Yet I thank the unknown supremo
For my tears hardened
Into granite chips,
For the flames that taught
The lessons of love and life
For his burning godhood
And your ice-cold humanity.

RACHEL BARI

HE WEPT

He wept
and
I
was lost
In
the intensity
of the emotion
I
could not
fathom

 He wept
as I
gathered
spoonsful
of puréed rice
to his open
mouth.
His brain
Sending
Signals
Slowly
Oh so
Slowly

He wept
I
did not
could not.

a
mute
being
with
no moorings.

He wept.
Papa
A lone tear
escaped his ninety
two years of
tired
eyelids.
His eyes
do not focus
My hand in his
as I support him
to stand tall
I remember
him holding me
When I fell

He wept.

I LOVE...

The supermarket was full
Reminding one of the latent fear
Lest the pandemic strikes again
The shelves were full, enticing
Customers, reassuring them
That this too shall pass
I picked up three big packets of
Maggi two minute noodles
The yellow one. the long one
A few more things, paid
And walked out, uncomfortable
With the congested space inside
The cold air outside was a relief
But the fear of COVID remained
The mask in place, socially distanced
I, on my scooter rode to deliver.
My father all of 92, lying on the divan
Gave me a toothless smile
I gestured that I had been out
To buy a few things, incomprehension
On his face and a query,
Until I turned, picked up Maggi
Showed it to him, the smile returned
I love Maggi ....he said

My world returned to normal
That toothless smile I shall cherish
Those lines will remind me
That in times of distress and distancing
You reassured me that in two minutes
One can find love.
This is for you Papa

LOPAMUDRA BASU

AT THE BORDER[2]

A short pudgy man with ice grey eyes once looked
at my papers, at the Ontario New York border and said
'You are missing one signature from the International Office.
I am not sure if you are a PhD candidate
or an illegal alien flipping burgers at McDonald's.'

The words sting, even after a decade, undeserved guilt,
raw fear of a life of many years,
rudely unravelling. A life spun in libraries,
rides on the uptown train to the Bronx,
our little apartment of ragged chairs, bookshelves bent
with secondhand books from the Strand, floors strewn
with essays of students who were single moms
juggling babies and exams, between flipping burgers.

A lifetime later, now with a new passport
my palms dampen and throat dries at the border.
I did not flee a war to come to this land,
with a toddler at my hip and my life in a backpack.
Yet I know that if this blue booklet with
the watermark of bald eagle is lost,
this face or accent will not shield me.

And if born in another country,
ruled by cartels instead of unions
I could be that woman at the border
hearing the last wail of a vanishing son
grief turning me to weeping stone like Niobe
or like Draupadi with matted hair mourning
the death of all her children in battle
or like Sethe, haunted by the ghost of Beloved,
death more bearable than children sundered by slavery.

WHITE ROSES

Today, I click on Kolkata Gifts Online and
order thirty white roses in a vase for you.
Ma sends me the photo of the roses
and tuberoses and the jasmine garland
all adorning your face today.

Two years ago, in that May of hell's heat and destruction
there were no garlands. Flower sellers
banished from the city like vermin thought to spread
the plague, dying of thirst on the way, walking hundreds
of miles, sometimes with no shoes.

Today, life goes on as usual in New York, New Delhi
and Kolkata— do people even remember that
there was no firewood or earth to bury the dead?
No flights from Minneapolis or Chicago
not even a phone call to hear you in the hospital.

We have said often that we have to think
of it as a natural disaster, an earthquake
or a cyclone like Amphan that tore you away
Except, it was not a forest fire and more
a Chernobyl with many forewarnings.

Two years later, so many names whispered
by the wind, and so many lives like leaves
blown away. So many souls still unmourned
and some like the white roses in the vase
pressed forever in memory's folds.

ARUNIMA BHATTACHARYA

MY NAME: ARUNIMA

'I am sorry I can't pronounce your name'.
The words were eyes on me.
It was the only name she could not, did not,
Say out loud.
My name—my hypertext link
Connecting to networks of familiarity and financial security
Is an error code.

Whenever my name is mispronounced, it rings alien to me
Something I want to disown.
I turn away from myself
I mimic the open quizzical gazes,
Stuck with a smile that is an apology
Also outrage.

Say my name.

Here my name trips and stutters in strange accents
There are a hundred permutations and combinations—
All familiar yet strange.
An approximate if not accurate gesture to conjure me.
It is hardly ever an easy job to say my name.
Deciphering the confusing sibilance of the 'n' and the 'm'

When my name is broken and lost
in a conversation,
I shrink a little,
folding myself into shapes
easy to read,
to remember.

My name makes for a difficult recall.
I am stuck with its intractability.

I can't refuse this gift from my mother.
Naming is an act of love, one of the firsts.
Yet I am exhausted by it.
Exhausted by the extra work I do
To be worth your effort of deciphering the consonants

I get stuck between correcting you and going along with it
Under a different sound I am still struggling to be myself
It is a reminder of unequal exchanges—
Across skin and citizenship.
It is a constant reminder,
That I am out of my element, where —
My name makes sense.
I am always difficult and foreign.

I feel like I am still not really here.

RADHA CHAKRAVARTY

SEVERED TONGUE[3]

They say proverbs are man-made.
They say wisdom is not for women.

But I defy their decree, and as a woman, speak
A different truth in a different tongue
that people can hear, when they hold their ear close
To the ground. My bold tongue speaks to them
Of soil, sky, sun, water, wind and rain
My voice smells of wet earth, manure and human toil.

I say—*Rain at winter's end signals a blessed land*
I say—*With willing hearts, even nine can share a bed*
I say—*For men cow-dung is toxic but for plants it's magic*
I say—*Plough when you have bulls or repent all year*
I say—*The croaking of frogs signals rain*
I say—*Rice grows in sunlight, but betel needs shade*

I speak the commonplace. The world listens. Like wildfire
through the land of Rarh, my words of wisdom spread.
I read the constellations, map the future in the sky.

Until Varahamihir, fabled star-gazer, star
of Chandragupta's court, trembles in rage and fear,
daunted by my dazzling auguries
That far outshine his own, casting
His pompous certitudes in doubt

Now they say, my tongue must be tamed.
They say, it's not my place to speak—
They say, a mere woman should be meek.

For reading the sky and searching the stars
For divining a different truth,
For enouncing the commonplace,
For taking knowledge to the folk,

I'm forced by them to sacrifice my tongue
Condemned to the fate of a silenced oracle …

But miracles will never cease! The severed tongue,
cut loose, assumes a life of its own,
bleeds new wisdom, which flows
like molten lava from my volcano soul.
My sayings spread through people's memories
and their hearts, across the lands, surging waves washing
over the hidden torrent of my tortured silence …

Silence of history, congealed, concealed
in an earthly mound in Rarh, remains, today, to remind
the curious visitor, that there once lived a woman,
Khona, whose incandescent words outlived
her deafening silence and outshone
those earthly stars, the powers that rule the world.
For her severed tongue bled and bled, and the blood spread,
sweeping
others into the flood, and the torrent of voices swelled, becoming
a rising tide of women, speaking, speaking, speaking out,
in many tongues*

* *"Severed Tongue" was first published in* Subliminal: Poems by Radha
  Chakravarty *(Hawakal Publishers, 2023.)*

WALKING THROUGH THE FLAMES

Walking through the flames,
she emerged unsinged.
And yet,
surely, Sita felt scorched within,
by the burning shame
of being put through the test,
ordeal by fire, before the gaze
of countless judging eyes,
appraising
her purity.
Outwardly unscathed, she survived,
yet, surely, something snapped
in Sita's heart that day,
her faith in faithfulness burned
to ashes by those accusing tongues of flame

When one day Sita called upon the earth
to open up and swallow her,
surely something should have changed for us,
forever?
After such bitterness,
Surely the world felt some shame?
Surely, things could never be the same
again, afterwards?
And yet ...*

* *'Walking Through the Flames' was first published in* Subliminal: Poems *by Radha Chakravarty (Hawakal Publishers, 2023).*

SANGEETA DEY ROY

GLORIFIED RED

Listening to the unintelligible mantras,
Her eyes gazed at the golden fire
The crackling of the twigs,
The pouring of the ghee,
As mantras bound them to be,
What society designed them to be.

She felt the feel of the red on her forehead—
The benchmark, the agreement
For the next phase of her life,
Of wifehood, daughter-in-law hood, motherhood.
She was told about her trajectory
And also the restraints in her region.
What followed were sober, crude colours
From the first bend.

The altar had actually glorified
Each petal of womanhood.
Which relayed a message,
"Rejoice in every compromise
And sacrifice you make ...
For these two virtues are seated in the
Highest pedestal of womanhood."

Sadly.... she failed to understand.

PRATHIM-MAYA DORA-LASKEY

ASIFA

Asifa died in January
it was April when I learned
it is always already too late
her body elegiac with pain

        don't call the police
        some of them raped her
        don't call god—his priest
        raped her in the temple

                she used to chirp
                like a bird her mother says
                but I keep hearing her cry
                hollow with hunger

        call the doctor
        they broke her legs
        call her parents
        she is eight

drugged then raped by men,
grown men, old men, men who
say to the father looking for her
"maybe she eloped?"

                she is eight. She goes
                looking for her horses
                we walk past to her river
                her horses, to our homes

we hear it is about religion
we hear it is about land
our thoughts catching
on branches of doubt

we know how in our
cruel, fool-ish world
land and religion erupts
on the soul of innocents

        there is her smiling face
        there is her stilled corpse
        in the same (only?) dress
        her silence becomes my voice

with all its broken bones
the secret, broken seams
dreaming of home, return-
ing to an unbroken body

        she knows more than I do
        and yet like any child asks
        why why why why why
        why why why why why

THE PRESENT

1.

thirteen years of this same name
with a few million different versions
to use in love, jokes, threats, loving

2.

when they decide for a new name
another parent tells me that a name
is like a present, no one has to like it

3.

just because you gave it to them...
they know what's best for them, they
get to decide if they want a new name.

4.

then they do decide for a new name—
"you know this name's unisex, right?"
"but—it still fits wrong," they say. So

5.

when they decided for a new name, I
find I'm delighted to have an excuse
to look at lists of baby names again

6.

with their new name, we learned they
can ask teachers to use the new one
but can't officially change it at school—

7.

that's another year with the same name
...but people ask us how to pronounce it
(because both names are from Sanskrit)

8.

we're tricksters this first year with the new
name: just tell them the old name is said
like the name you picked, I say. I'm loved

9.

more in this first year with their new name
it's like they spread their prayers like wings
these are small things, but they can fly now

10.

when they decided on this new name, I...
was really relieved the new name began
kind of same way that their old one did—

11.

so in this first year with the new name—
I can catch myself before I land wrong.
"Doesn't Elliot Page have a name like that?"

12.

"I don't even remember"—they're saying—
what it was, they're in the present; I'm
rewarded with them happy in this year

13.

with just a new name

ARRANGED MARRIAGES
FOR TEEN DEVIS

Note: The structure of the poem mimics the shifting rift between different generations with parallel columns growing closer and coagulating in each section.

(First, the disappeared grandaunt)

Suseela, grandaunt	she only came to be, came to me
(grandaunt, yes, but when	because Amma read
she died she's younger than I am	Maxine Hong's Kingston's
when I first hear of her)	*No Name Woman*
Suseela who had been sent off	and whispered there's a woman
to college for a year	we do not talk about
and then married off	in our family too

turn the page turn the corner	what is the good death
of the year, watch her she returns	is it in the child planted
from her husband's house	in the dirt of her body
where they will not let her read	planted, fruiting, frightening
with bruises painted on her arms	what do you know of ghosts
her teeth crooked from resistance	the ghosts jailed in your body

watch her return to her mother	her feet planted at the well
return to her father's house	clutching her hair, her hope
who had said:	seeing miracles
only your dead body	babbling in prayer
should ever leave	as if anyone is listening
your husband's house	as if they ever listen

well... there's a well	a pulley to pull water
the family well	it pulls time out of her
poisoned now by her dead body	it takes all her remaining years
drowning in memories	though few remember

(Then, the pregnant, unmarried aunt)

Leela, aunt like a sister to my mother
like another mother I fed you from my breasts
she likes to rest her hand she likes to say
on my head gesturing at her breasts
tell me she felt me dance making me look
before I was born laughing as my eyes drop
when she was pregnant too and my color rises

her love so intense it must have in a desert with
felt like devastation no rain no rain
to whom could she give that love only her thirst

I want to ask her how in a world it would be water
where girls like her were watched it would be thirsty
so closely she managed to get it would be wet
pregnant before she was married needing release
as if by the bogey lovers her teeth playful and crooked
her father imagined and feared from lying through them

Leela, so open so lonely if she were born today
So lovely so open she'd be flying her dupatta
So lonely like a flag as she sailed
So lonely away on a moped
No one cared and no one would care

(And just before my parents' arranged marriage)

when my mom was trying hard to be my best friend
(so I too would share, so I wouldn't decide to die)
she once told me how in the late sixties
she'd take the 21 bus from her college
to go "flirt" at the university library

heading home meant rules and four younger siblings
(and college was only to make her marriage worthy)
so she'd stay back to read trashy novels
knowing dudes were watching her
from neigh- boring desks

I feel a flicker for mom in her carefully pressed saris
(pressed under her mattress if she missed the dhobi)
knowing she'd never   be allowed to work
using the few   years she had
for freedom,   for fun

she told me she never looked directly at any of them
(I mean, that would be   to risk a bad reputation)
but there was one   bespectacled dude
who seemed   a very serious type
she didn't   know his name

graduation results went up, and he asked how she did
(she was too taken by   surprise to counterfeit, so)
she told him she got   a third class—i.e. a "C"
he turned on his heel   —and she laughs—
she never   saw him again

TISHANI DOSHI

TIGER WOMAN[4]

after a nineteenth-century Mughal painting of two men
in pursuit of a tiger woman

No one writes poems for the handsome sidekick
who barely makes the frame—there to collect his master's
clothes by the river. He has seen those creamy, solid thighs
a thousand times, knows what lies behind the shrubs
of pink—body bags, flies. You would rather hear
about the woman, the chimera beneath. You want to know
what the air was like that febrile day, how the sun crafted
a way to shine upon her fan of hair. I understand. You would
rather talk about the things only you can see—
the tiger paws, the tail, a body transformed underwater.
But if you listen to the sidekick, he can tell you why all the old cities
made fortresses of themselves, how those soft, green mounds
evocative of breasts should have been painted as ruined blocks
of apartments instead. You do not get to have an empire
without squashing someone else. Lean in and he will tell you how
the summer hunts are so frequent, even the heap of muslin
on the bank is overcome with sweat. Even the cicadas
who are sawing the afternoon in half seem to be signaling a threat.
On this occasion, the tiger woman escapes, but the sidekick
knows, eventually the body fails. How many times
has he found himself dreaming of bird feet and a plumed tail?
Some way to take flight. You see, the river is sweet
and brims with carp, but the water's edge is
skin, stained with curses and blood sacrifices.
In one part of the world something is always blooming.
No amount of washing takes the smell off him. *

**"Tiger Woman" was commissioned by the Royal Academy of Arts Magazine in 2020.*

POOJA GARG

DEHISCENCE

(1)

Mother is a doctor. She says Eat

for my skin to become smooth, for my

muscles to turn firm, for my

bones to grow strong

Eat, eat, eat she says,

hurriedly now

looking at the door,

Now looking at the garage,

Now looking at the garage door opening

Now looking at the garage door closing,

Now looking at my father coming in,

Now my father bringing my plate to me

Eat, eat, eat he says,

slowly now

So slowly it soothes after mother's incessant rush

So slowly he puts the plate down

So slowly he puts his hands on my face

S o   s l o w l y — I   d o n't   s e e   theslapcoming

For my smooth skin, my firm muscles, my strong bones

To

c

r

u

m

b

l

e

now now now.

(2)

Dad is an engineer. He says Learn coding,

Learn binary:

One and Zero

Yes and No

He says Yes, we are

One income family, Zero

contribution from mother.

                She says No, she

                cooks, cleans, takes

                care of me:

Yes, Yes, Yes, I say clutching her hand

No—

my binary father says, as she

                is pushed to the wall, No

                as she is taken to the hospital, No

                as she returns

This time to say Yes—

(3)

I was sure he was my friend. I knew it

because we shared

                the bus

the classroom

                the table at lunch time

I knew it definitely

because he did not call my lunch smelly

when I opened my box of lemon rice from home

and also because he said I was smart

So when he asked for my notes, I gave them to him—

I gave them to him again

when he was out for a match

when he had a date

when he went on holiday

He even had my notebook in his bag

the day he called me his Indian slave

in a voice that echoed down

the bus, the classroom, the lunch table—

SHWETA RAO GARG

~~SURPANAKHA'S~~ MEENAKSHI'S RANT

Don't you bother with this name.
My nails are shapely and long
Done at the best salons
To fit me into the script,
I was made the classic Other
My name's Meenakshi—fish-shaped-eyes—
I don't eat people for lunch; I prefer rice.
Years ago, in the woods, I saw a man I desired
As a woman to a man, I propositioned
He seemed amused and shook his head
Was he too vain? I couldn't tell.
Pointed to the lady next to him
"I'm content with one wife
The man yonder has known no pleasure
Offer yourself to my brother."
I'd agreed to the decision,
The other man had the same disposition
But he passed me in turn
Like I was a plaything
I saw the men smirk
The woman stared at me
With revulsion,
I decided to teach them a lesson
I charged at her,
Before I knew it, I felt my hair pulled
I pleaded to let me go
They wanted to hurt me more;
"How do we punish her; do I chop off her ears
Or shall I settle for her nose?"

I writhed, I kicked, I shrieked
Then I smelled iron,
The last thing I will ever smell.

Later I discovered these men's history
When I was told about Ayomukhi
I heard that she had died from sepsis
And perhaps also of a broken heart.
I got off relatively easy with an injury
I moved on after the war
Though haunted with guilt
Rhinoplasty was affordable
After years of thrift
My nose is still numb
But sometimes I think
I can still whiff the smell
Of my blood mingled with rejection.

ROOPALI SIRCAR GAUR

PHILOMELA: TODAY, YESTERDAY AND TOMORROW[5]

If you cut off a woman's tongue
like they did the other day
in that dusty dirty town of Hathras
in India then at the dead of night you must
incinerate whatever remains of her.
Her broken spine, her lacerated vagina
and her mutilated soul.

In another age Greek King Tereus of Thrace
Also could not contain his lust
and ravished and violated Philomela
she won't be silent she had said
so, with pincers he held her tongue
and with a sharp sword
he cut off her tongue.

Philomela's anguish did
not hold back her story
her aching fingers wove an intricate tapestry
unfolding a tale with images telling
Just like poets tell our stories.

A stunned avenging sister Procne
cooked and served in an ornate dish
a depraved dinner fit for a King
their only son Ity's flesh
a father and a rapist husband
King Tereus of Thrace.

The head paraded for proof
silenced forever the
raging perpetrator.
The voiceless nightingale granted
a voice to lament Philomela's sorrow.

Will the many gods of our people
 let us write our legends?
can we tell our tales?
How else will the soulful chronicles be told
of Antiope, Hera, Europa and Leda
Medusa, Draupadi and Sita,
Hannah, Regina, Jyoti and Shaheena
all ravaged, mutilated and morphed
by Zeus, Poseidon, Duryodhan and Ravana
Jean clad Sandeep, Herbert Mike and Mirza.

Must we then like Procne
avenge feed the flesh
of sons to fathers.

BITOO'S MOTHER

Bitoo's mother washes dirty dishes in lalaji's house.
chewed chicken bones left over potato pieces
on the nausea piled plate she takes home with her
wrapped in her damp saree the stale stench of leftover food.

Some smells bring memories
of her clinging to mother's saree
and the never forgotten angry voice, "again you have brought
her with you!"
The voice echoed her sad childhood never allowing her to bring
the pleading Bitoo along.
Lalaji's wife was kind she sometimes gave her the broken bis-
cuit pieces left in the tin and
on Diwali a box of ladoos. Her mother had also collected smells.

The Sudarshan Chakra looking Corona chased thousands like her
over many barefoot miles towards the yellowing sugarcane fields.
In the smoke of the dusty city, she had forgotten home.

Bitoo fell asleep on Lalaji's
battered red suitcase
trundling wobbly wheels
singing a lullaby on the melting
hot tar road.
Whirring TV channels
like alien flying saucers
brought the stoic exodus
into our air-conditioned homes
    making us very angry and the hungry thirsty road days gave
way to oily fried puris and
cool bottles of mineral water!
When the gaunt faces and
shrunken bellies could not smile
for the selfies we muttered "ungrateful wretches".

The sleeping child on the suitcase had become the brand of an
exhausted Pandemic panic.
Nobody knew it was Bitoo.

His mother's saree no longer smelt of Lalaji's dirty dishes
the hot summer wind had blown it all away.
They were going home.

ANUJA GHIMIRE

ABOUT LOVE, OR I WISH OUR MOTHERS COMPLAINED MORE

my mother used to blame in couplets
said she fought with life and death
to give birth three times
and I scoffed *everyone does that*
she was too young to be a mother
milk teeth memory intact
I found her old enough to battle at twenty-six
my mother guilted in idioms
about stones in lentils, defiant cats,
and the numbering of days after death
in a dialect I half understood,
only the complaints of children
who *could have used punishment*, she would laugh
I wanted my mother to be someone else
her ways of love something else
not the mango juice box she dropped off at noon
in a pressed silk sari and cherry red lipstick,
on her way home from half day at work
left foot half escaping the two-inch heel
not the haircut she asked the algebra teacher
to try to coax me into getting
a failed formula of only wrong answers
I had just learned embarrassment
a shade of shame, a compound of my feelings
tainted by others when my beautiful mother
was on the other side of the primary class door
and disregard of care, my mother's,
unwanted in her manner of delivery
all the regrets are dead stars still aglow
I am fighting with pride
and guilt to be born again

BHASWATI GHOSH

NAVIGATION

You came with varied geographies
on your face. I was exhausted from
birthing, but not enough to stop
speculating on the amusing afterlife
the maps on your visage would assume.

Inside me throbbed the song of busy
cicadas, its tenor nippy, its notes
shrill with the sureness of a just-failed
marriage. My bed, neither wide nor rosy
needed to hold your tiny frame and

my head, big with worry. Turns out you
and I had the same forte. We knew survival.
On a horizon as blurry as my job prospects,
we coursed our way with the theatrical
ecstasy of dancing on a crooked road.*

* *'Navigation' was published in Bhaswati Ghosh's debut collection of poems* Nostalgic for a Place Never Seen *(Copper Coin, 2024).*

MANDIRA GHOSH

KAFKA'S WORLD[6]

Smell of death fills the air
Smell of dead bodies, dead bones
Bodies fainted in Ventilators
OTs
Like frogs in the wax-board
Ready for dissection.

Morbid evenings
condemn the virus
Man waits in the crematoriums
Doesn't touch his son's body
Cremations if possible are unattended
Funerals are without relatives.
All wail without touching others....

It is Kafka's world.
Camus cries as he is powerless
Facing distress and destiny
................in a morbid, distraught world.

Then from cities survivors move to nowhere
Entire livings on their cycles
Wife delivers the baby on the street.
Whom to blame, only God can send remedies!

Oh! Krishna we all know that the soul is immortal

But can you tell us
where are they moving?
Towards which destinations?
Unknown destinations

Migration to their homes?

Migrants marching.

Indeed marching
Before another battle begins...

ZERBANOO GIFFORD

ALMOST MY MOTHER

For my godmother Maperviz

My Mother's best friend died today—
she was my darling Godmother.
My ritual was to speak to her
every morning before going to work.
I had to catch her before
she started her daily prayers,
across time zones—
hours ahead of me,
She in Pune, India
I, in the Forest of Dean,
in my precious ASHA center,
my brainchild
in the midst of the U.K.

I needed her prayers
I needed funding
It was floundering.

Aah my ASHA center
Founded by me,
Is close to my heart,
in the lush forest of Dean
a place of enlightenment and connection
to nature, self, and others.
For many young people,
from all over the world,
it is paradise.
A place to prepare for life not death.

My Godmother said "Pray for yourself,
as you know, no one, not even God,
says NO to you.
Everyone loves you."

Irritated I explained I don't know how to pray.
The last thing she said to me,
was just try.

My godmother's name was the beautiful Persian name Maperviz,
"first star of the night".
As a little girl I couldn't spell.
I wrote to her every week from my boarding school and could
only go as far as MAP
So everyone called her MAP.
When people change their names, they take on a new life.
I don't know whether I changed her life, but she was at the heart
of mine.
They say death of a loved one is the worst trauma
we little mortals must endure.
My head is still flashing with my life with an old soul.
She has returned to the stars in the sky from where she and we
all come from.
I am left just looking at the stars.
Will I see her tonight?

NANDINI GUHA

SILENCE OF SORROW

Untimely death shattered my life like a bombshell.
The trauma of unending responsibilities loomed ahead of me
They weighed down heavily on my lonely shoulders.

Yet in me arose the determination not to cry and break down
To remain calm in the face of
emotional stress and mental confusion.

The need to look forward not backward.
The decision to conduct my daughter's wedding
in a way that no one could show pity
for a fatherless child.

The dedication to care for an aging mother
who had been dealt the cruelest blow of all.

Then one day came the easing of tension
When both children at long last
were standing on their own two feet.

Came the joy of grandchildren and work satisfaction
The relief of knowing my responsibilities
were finally coming to an end.

I spent twenty-three years with my husband.
Today I have lived without him
for the same number of years.

Have I lost or gained in life?
Only my Maker can tell.

RENU GUPTA

LOVE, LOST (SELF-TRANSLATION FROM THE ORIGINAL WRITTEN IN HINDI)

प्रेम,

एक दुनिया

जो हम दोनों से, हम दोनों के बीच, बस जाती है।

उस शहर की सब राहें

हम दोनों को पास ही लाती है।

वहां, हर मोड़, हर दर, हमारा अपना है।

आने वाले कल के सभी सपने, सभी आँगन,

हम साथ साथ जोड़ते रहते हैं।

और जो यूँ ही बसते-बसते

कायनात

बंजर हो जाए ?

कितने ही शहर बसें, कितनी ही गलियाँ चुनें,

और हमारी ड्योढ़ी न रचे ?

तो बटोर कर किस कोने में रख आएँ

वो प्रेम जिसका कोई घर-आँगन नहीं?

अब

तुम्हारी आँखों में मेरी परछाइयाँ भी मायूस हैं।

बेचारगी का शोर

तुम्हारी रूह की गहराईयों से उठकर

मेरी नस-नस में उतर गया है

जिस तरह कभी मुस्कराहट उतरती थी तुम्हारी।

अब,

प्रेम

जैसे प्रेत हो कोई।

Love,
gives birth to a whole new world—
for us, from us.
All the paths in that universe,
are mere bridges that only get us closer,
each turn, each door, belongs to us.
All the dreams of tomorrow and each bustling courtyard,
we keep weaving together.
And if,
all of this world just turns barren overnight?
no matter how many more worlds are born and reborn,
our thresholds just turn to dust before we even come across to
hold each other?
How do I gather and where do I bury
all the love that now has nowhere to belong?
Now,
shadows of our loss lurk in your eyes,
screams of helplessness have penetrated my being passing
through your soul,
the way your smile used to once.
Now love
is just a ghost.

DELLNAZ WADIA ITALIA

THAT TWITCH

I stand on a carcass.
There's steel, concrete, bricks
crushed mortar, wires, switches
and a dirty yellowing thing that twitches.
I step closer.
Walk gingerly on the carcass
of a stubby building
razed to the ground.
A balcony with wooden banisters
a parapet with chiseled cherubs
is now a sawdust mound.
Shards of painted panes glint
in the harsh summer sun.
The stubby building lies lifeless—
It is just a heap of glitches.

That Twitch bewitches.
You can't go there; it isn't safe.
The architect cautions.
His voice doesn't reach.
That Twitch reaches.
It is twitching peevishly
as if its very life force is depleted.
It extends its furl to me.
I hold it.
The Twitch is a yellow handkerchief
that used to be white
I free it
from the tile that held its end captive.
It twitches in my hand.

It transports me to a sunny afternoon
Long gone before fifty cycles of the moon.
I can feel my daddy fish into his pocket.
 bring out this white Twitch.
He rubs the trails of fresh, alphonso ice cream
trickling down my greedy mouth.
We smile at each other with our very bellies.
The stubby building smiles at us.
It houses us into its cool shadow.

The stubby building is a carcass.
The daddy is long gone.
The ice cream has melted into an Alphonso* memory.
The tall building will be erected soon.
I clutch the dirty, yellowed handkerchief
in my clammy palm.
It twitches.

* 'Alphonso' is one of the many variants of the Indian mango.

JAYSHREE IYER

ORPHANED (INSPIRED BY THE CONTROVERSY OVER THE CITIZENSHIP AMENDMENT ACT IN INDIA)[7]

You want proof of my Indianness.

Can you not see it in the sweat of my brow?
Can you not feel it in these calloused hands?
in the wear and tear of my mind and body
to field, factory, office and home?

Can you not hear it in my accent;
in its rising and falling inflections
and in the way my 'w' is a 'v'
And my 't' a 'd'?

Can you not feel it in the cool bright cottons I wear
to match my wheatish complexion
in the searing sun?
Can you not hear it in the familiar filmy songs I hum?
Can you not taste it in the fingers that scoop daal, chawal and achaar
and in the sweet milky chai that scorches my lips?

Every breath I take
Every tear I shed
Every sigh I let out
Screams
I am Indian
And still
You want proof of my Indianness.

The soil that nurtured me
is stained with my blood
And soiled with your scorn.

What do you do
when the sea turns its back on the river?
when the banyan withholds its shade?
Where do you go
when the father disowns his child
and the mother pushes it away from her bosom?

Is there
a documentation for despair
a land for the orphaned
a refuge from loneliness?

Will there ever be a boundary to contain pain?

ZILKA JOSEPH

IF I GIVE ALL I POSSESS TO
THE POOR AND GIVE OVER MY BODY
TO HARDSHIP

—CORINTHIANS 1

the shriveled human-like corpse
a shell of a body in rags we saw
sprawled on our landing
when we came home one night
the small thin creature lying limbs
akimbo looked like a teenaged boy
wearing shorts and had short spiky hair
mouth fallen open
drool leaking in bubbles
from cracked lips

we gasped
it was a woman torn
apart and left to die or sleep
we saw that a dirty white T-shirt
three times her size was pulled up
to her chin and her filthy khaki
shorts ripped off her skin and bone
body and her knobbly legs
shoved apart and the darkness
that lay there between those thighs
more ravaged than her skin

her eyes were turned up as if she were
searching for something we could not see

we could see the whites of her eyes
her neck arched off the concrete floor
drug addict my father said quickly
as he tried to shield my mother
my sister and I from the sight
edged us away from her unmoving body
unlocked our door and shoved us
inside our flat and turned the key
then ran to call the local watchman

but I had seen the crumpled rupees
in her fist tightly clenched
as if in the throes of death
she clung to what might
feed her for yet another day

SOUNDING BRASS AND TINKLING CYMBALS WITHOUT LOVE

—CORINTHIANS 1

even now I hear her tinny bangles jingle
see the fake gold earrings shimmer

was it her father or husband or brother or uncle
who tricked her

who sold her
who the middle-man
who the pimp
who the betrayer
the betrayed

how many times a night did
they tear into her flesh there
in the alcove or on the landing
near the terrace above us
or perhaps right outside our door
or on the neighbor's filthy mat
did he maybe watch
lecher that he was

how much did they pay the police
our landlord the local thugs
how much did God/the gods
hear and see and witness
surely everything

and just like us ran away
to save ourselves

we *see no evil hear no evil speak no evil*
we saved ourselves

from goondas
from the almighty God/gods
(is there a difference)
and did nothing to save the girl

FEROZA JUSSAWALLA

THE DIVORCE DISLOCATION

Kilauea is erupting again,
Hawaiian eruptions, I have personified,
taken into my body,
like the eruptions
of rancid acid,
from my own gut,
through my hiatal hernia,
opening like the mouth of Kilauea
drowning me,
in my own fluids,
undigested food,
undigestable announcements
filling my lungs—
drowning me
interstitial lung disease
from the day you erupted
with your divorce announcement
turning me to limpid lava,
drowning me—

But Madame Pele
awakens me,
from my chemo fog
to dance in my own fire.

Hawaii, where my mother had moved,
when cast out of our motherland
nineteen seventy-six, Emergency
turned, bicentennial year of hospitality.

Hawaii, what I thought was my *aina*
and you, you, husband of thirty years,
cast me out again,
locations, dislocations,
continuous and constant,
movements and migrations,
every one of them, cancerous
from Las Cruces, to Albuquerque,
to Hawaii and back to Albuquerque.

And you, you as you parade in your
academic regalia, well lei'd,
as I watch from behind
a chain link fence,
unacknowledged,
in my own mother's land
that she brought you to,
where you parade with
another woman,
well lei'd.

That gut punch
you dealt me husband,
has turned into hernias
hiatal, inguinal,
strangulated
bowels of pain,

Thirty years of service
to you,
husband,
where did they go?

FRACTURED

A purple pensiveness
falls over me, as I
contemplate
fractured bodies
and purple passions.

Who will love me now,
at sixty-six,
with lumpectomied
one and half breasts
and a bulging
inguinal hernia
caused by
moving boxes
after the radical hysterectomy
of cancers past.

None will hold women
broken and fragmented,
afraid to touch
cracked glass,
like shards of crystal glassware,
resulting from being,
dropped in the deliberate abandonment
of betrayals, wrought
by those who should have loved us.

Why do we submit?
to fracturing?

Grief is too painful to contemplate
in purple pensiveness.

Can we be Kintsugi'd?
Using gold, to fill the cracks
of my life, has become
too burdensome—

I will remain, "feroza",
scarred with pyrite,
copper turquoise,
they call it in India,
Nishapuri, like my
Persian origins,
Sonoran gold,
in my new desert home,
where sand pours through cracks
like a sieve,
unrepairable!

SONIAH KAMAL

EVENING OF THE 4TH OF JULY

She applies lipstick
to her
reflection in
the dark of the
computer monitor
her face
the bones of shadow
play
the color
mute
as she drags a red pencil
she'd brought from the
dollar store clearance bin
to keep her lips
in
though she will
fill them up
like padded bosoms
with a clear plumping serum
that shines
and winks
no matter how
dark the screen
that conceals
the peacock blue and green;
the bruiser kiss
She did not want
she could not stop.

DEAR DESI MOTHERS

Stop coercing your daughters.
Stop telling them to smile for the camera.
Don't turn them into robots if they
don't say cheese to please.
Stop emotionally blackmailing your daughters.
Stop manipulating your daughters.
Into getting married to anyone at all.
Into doing your bidding.
Into living nightmares to fulfill
Your dreams.
You had your chances. You didn't take them.
Stop sacrificing your daughters to
Society Gods.
Stop telling them life begins after marriage.
Stop worrying them about marriage.
Stop harping about 'age' and 'duty' and 'breaking your heart'.
They are not your servant, your best friend, your property and,
above all, they are
Not your parent.
You are the parent which means acting with maturity and not
like a brat
throwing tantrums or silent treatments or
other forms of
emotional coercions and crookedness.
On camera everything is brighter
On camera everyone dresses up
On camera everyone buttons up
On camera everyone behaves
On camera everyone smiles
when they are told to smile
On camera even our
teeth smile
On camera our smiles
Don't bite.

AMRIT KAUR

A FIRE OF JUSTICE BURNING BRIGHT

She stands strong, a pillar of fire
Her strength has no expiration
An unstoppable force, inspiring us all
To turn passion into action.
Fearless in her quest for justice
And to rise up against the tide
A light in her eyes that no darkness can dim
A zenith of womanly pride.
Let us trumpet the call of justice and fairness
And share the message far and wide;
Forward we march with her light to guide us—
Her emboldened spirit, our stride.

RATIKA KAUSHIK

SORRY FOR SURVIVING

Darwin came knocking.
Spoke of survival,
Only the fittest survives.
The one who adapts, the one who bends and the one who changes.
Survives, may be not thrive, but survives.

Locked in the pandemic, we needed to survive.
We needed to eat.
Some needed to be fed.
We needed to check O2 levels.
We needed to wash hands, as often and as hurriedly as beavers always wanting to clean themselves.
We needed to just about survive.

I told Darwin,
That your theories don't fit.
It is May 2020,
And the fittest haven't survived.

I am the fittest cook, cleaner, helper and caregiver before 9am, and the most excited professor till 3pm.
After 3pm, starts another round of cooking, cleaning, feeding the children and caregiving.
And it never stops. But I survive with heavier heart and lighter Earth, I survive.

But I survive, just until midnight; I am drowned in the silences of children sleeping.

The days go hazy and dull. Smothered in anxiety and stuffed with food, I survive.
I understand, having a roof over my head is a gift. I do. But this roof will fall over me someday.
A comfortable bed, a fridge full of food, a job that pays, all this be a privilege, Mr. Darwin.

But my mind wanders away, and my soul cringes at this monotony.
Survival shouldn't be so hard, and the scars of survival should faint away with time.
Yet every breathing human is accepting these survival scars that are yet to scab,
For a bonus life of injections, medicines, masks, and fewer loved ones.

COVID gets a new survival rate every day and we are peeking through margins, adjusting new realms.
I am not unhappy that I wake up to see a new dawn, believe me Mr. Darwin.
I am not the fittest, yet I survive.
I am sorry for surviving to see that outside my door, breathing beings will be less, not more.

HAFIZA NILOFAR KHAN

TRAUMATIZED IN DHAKA

I don't know what causes a bigger trauma—
Grade 3 Anaplastic Meningioma
Invading your brain
In some Iowan hospital, hotel, then hospital again?

Or the lingering words chewing my membrane—
"Marriage is a mere contract.
And a very restraining institution, for that"
Uttered so nonchalantly, as you left?

I don't know what causes a bigger trauma—
You at the mercy of the precise rays
Zapping through your skull
Maiming your left arm and right leg?

Or, not knowing where I stand—
Married, divorced or just a friend
After thirty plus years
Of being a lover, a wife, a mother?

I don't know what causes a bigger trauma—
Faces of friendships you pursued
In the name of humanity, charity, empathy
But served your altruistic ego, accrued?

Or, medical debts looming large,
Lawyer, court fees or alimony
If I initiate what you desired:
A severing of ties; a death decree?

I don't know what causes a bigger trauma—
Seeing a home I craved in America
Harboring homegrown terrorists
And partaking in Muslim genocide?

Or, drowning in an abysmal Bangladesh
That kills Ethics at every turn
Adulterating food, polluting environment,
Constructing, deconstructing for no return?

SUDIPA LAMA

WILLIWAW*—A POINT OF RETURN

Alive, I am today,
Yesterday, I was just living.
Nine winters passed by, to realize,
Shelley's optimism for spring.

The courage I least had,
Footsteps fumbling, Hands trembling.
 Faith low, Willpower weak,
I was on the nadir.

I needed buoyancy, But heavy,
Like an iron tied on my feet,
Refraining to be blameworthy,
I was immersed fully.

Anxiety grew, Depressed,
Pills on pills I lived,
Hemlock, I drank,
Sick and dry—A living cactus.

Immunity weak, The pandemic on the rise,
Crying and wailing,
Passing my days,
My heart and brain less functioning.

I only had a shoulder to cry, Pacing me up,
Oh! Those dire days,
 I hardly want to think.
The deadly virus gulped me...

Suffocated I lived, death so near,
But the depression vanished and the anxiety too.
Delusively, the infirmary became my hospice,
Off base, for sure was a zenith for me.

 I swear, I had the manna and the ambrosia there,
Like a warrior with his weapon stacked,
Basking with my return,
I was the Lazarus—Comeback from the dead.

Half year passed by then,
Adjusting with being the Sylvia's Lady Lazarus,
My world came crushing down,
With the loss of my creator and his forebear.

Indeed! The loss is immeasurable, I can hardly define.
And time, like cheetah runs clueless,
Resuming my sail to honor my creator in heaven,
 Nevertheless with my ambition strong, hurdling, I am sailing.

I am buoyant now, not like a corpse.
But living and dead are
the critics,
For I have my shoulder holding me still,
And bulwark strong.

With a hurdle down among many,
I am living.
I am living.
I am living.

---

* Williwaw is an Alaskan term for a strong, cold wind, bringing disaster to the coastal and mountainous region of Alaska.

SEETHA LAKSHMI

TO GROW UP AS CLOSETED DALIT QUEER IN INDIA'S METROPOLITAN CITY

My Father moved to the city when I was one
Socially deprived and controlled me and my mother
Like we were his possessions to own
I was always seen as a Dalit girl in his eyes
Which made him hypervigilant
The sense of purity and how I don't look or seem
Like a normal girl
Was imbibed in every word and action

To sit comfortably
As a Dalit daughter
Was called being a rebel
Coupled with guilt trips
Of not being a good girl

I didn't know any better
Than to listen to my instincts—
That completely contradicted patriarchy
My instincts were always
Not just unacknowledged
But shamed and guilted
Thus unexpressed

To the point I never could
Trust myself ever
Never could I relate
To another

Never felt I belonged
To a place
Never relaxed
In my own body

To put my love
In words or actions
Has not been the easiest
For I was not modelled
To express my emotions—
Let alone in a healthy way.

Becoming an adult body possessed by
A very disturbed abandoned child
Carrying on generations of trauma and
Breaking the cycle... I search for solace...
For peace
In myself—amidst displacements, insecurities and toxic links

For this body and soul saw too much too soon
The mind and nervous system is still processing
To adapt to reality, with glitches
It's bound to show up as symptoms

And in me
I see
The child
That yearned so much
To be free
And why can't I be?
—is a work in progress
And knowing I won't
Abandon myself.

LALITA LIMBU

MY RELATIONSHIP WITH COLOR[8]

Have you ever,
Thought about the relationship with your favourite color?
I never did because I never enjoyed harmony with colors.
Some people ask me with excitement, "What's your favorite
color?"
Bewildered, I ask myself, "What is my favorite color?"
White, black, red, purple, green or any other?
No colors come to mind
I am bewildered
I am speechless
Truthfully, I don't have any favorite color.
Just like with colors, I don't have harmonious relations with my
memories.
Loud voice, leather boot, the color red, navy blue uniform, dark
cave, height, big boulder and many more.

I don't quite recall, it may be around 2002
My childhood filled with mischief and curiosity
The buds of curiosity snatched without letting them bloom
The desire to play, stroll around, wander freely charged by fear
Fueled by current affairs and hourly NEWS bulletins aired on
Radio Nepal
The Royal Nepal Army clashed with Maoist rebels in Rukum,
death and injuries piled up
In the East and in the West, in my backyard too
Leaving an indelible mark on my tender childhood???

They are still fresh in the cabinet of memories,
As my mother, father, aunt and uncles conversed and discussed
politics around the fire late into the night

I revelled in their conversations,
Until one day they came to an abrupt stop
As relatives and neighbors stopped visiting,
One by one
Madan Mela (carnival) where long distant relatives, friends and lovers met, was abandoned
Sankranti Bazaar, a lively village market and trading post, fell silent
The Dhan Naach (harvest dance) where young men and women courted disappeared.
The celebratory and joyous Dhol Naach (Drum Dance) was lost
The open field near our house where children used to play became deserted.
Their voices, their songs, the songs of lovers lost
Replaced by harsh violent sounds, reverberating
People beating people
The rising death toll of guilty and innocent making headlines for days.

One Day while returning from school, young brother and sisters ahead, a group of older brothers behind,
Suddenly, a huge bomb exploded on top of the hill
Gunshots rained down incessantly
"Save me, I am dying", cries for help
We screamed in fear, the older brothers begging us not to run
Away from the creek
Hands shaking, fearful tears running down our cheeks, we raised our hands like criminals
And, the colorful sky above us
Became innocent

The next day, a lifeless corpse lying in the woods near the school
The ground covered with bullet holes and blood
Me, an innocent witness,
I cannot describe the pain.
I started at every small sound
I feared vibrant colors,
I hid in a corner when someone came to my house
I feared the big boulder, the dark cave, even from afar,

I should have been happy with friends, became a loner instead.
My joyous childhood scarred by the momentous event
Distancing myself from society.

Days and month passed by, the years too
Decades later
I start and tremble at the sound of thunder in the sky
A reminder in the still of night of those dark times
Flashes reflected in the colorful sky

What should I say
Colors at times
Return me to my childhood
A sorrowful moment, an unwelcome gift

SHYAMASRI MAJI

THE HOME-GOING BUS
IN THE TIME OF COVID-19

There is no shoulder to weep upon,
no shoulder to carry the corpse
I left my baggage in the broken bridge
chasing the home-going rush

I ran for the bus, the last one, they said,
was about to leave in quarter of an hour.
Panting for breath, I reached the stand—
The crowd, the virus, I said, "Aghast!"

A cop—a young lady—upright and strong,
she led me through the unfeeling throng,
We looked at each other to unscrew time
Summer clouds swayed like scent of lime
Doffing my mask, nervously I did ask—
"Are you not our sweeper Mani's daughter?"

Nodding her head with meek affirmation,
she replied, "Sister, I am Moyna,
the girl you send to high school,
Arguing with your father, Mr. Raina"

I looked at the sky.
Soon it was to be dusk.
Yet, so much was left to say and ask:
Who stole the butterflies from the cupboard of my rainbow?
Who smelt the coconut sweets on my adolescent window?
And many more to pry on...

Once the door of home is ajar!

The bus conductor called.
The fuming wheels furrowed the breezy stretch of sand,
she waved at me and I smiled back to her.

In the guilty glow of the lantern sky
the bus took a turn and gathered speed,
I longed to hold her tough and deep arms
beckoning at me with a tilted hourglass

LOVESTORIYAN

Many times, I fell down in love
a felled tree chopped from its trunk
Under the hooting sky, now—

Lovers crawl on my bark,
their faces die in the dark.
A poison flower blooms on my tattooed breast,
my navel fumes, lava flows from its crest.
Sweet air that swayed the roses once
pelts my skin with a thorny glance.

Teardrops whirl in a bathing tub,
 I lay awake like a fluorescent bulb.
Staring at the sleeping man,
the night flutters under the ceiling fan.
I turn the dry leaves of a yellow past
recalling the seasons that decayed fast.
Tonight, love settles like frost on a sheaf,
watching the moon with the scorn of a thief.

SHIKHA MALAVIYA

HIRAETH

After Nirbhaya

*You are the one with more than one name: Braveheart,
Lightening, Fearless One. A star is a star is a star is
a star. Is what you are. Aspiring astronomer's dream,
galactic dirge, lover's requiem.*

Celestial layers crumble at the touch, scattering savoury star-
dust. Travelling at the speed of light, you halt in front of a ham-
mock made of stars. Soul pinballing through the universe, zig
zag zoom, Mars to Jupiter to Neptune, you break off a corner
from Saturn's rings. Too salty you think, as it falls through your
tongue. Touch is taste and taste is touch. 5-4-3-2-1. The black hole
unfurls its movie screen to show big and little bangs. Today, the
movie is you. The body you carefully maintained, oiled, plucked,
rubbed, anointed, scrubbed—undone by a thread's pull, the sil-
ver one binding you to earth, broken by betelnut stained canines.
They bite into you tasting type-A blood and like plaster of Paris
the skin holds impressions, soaked with local hooch and seasonal
employment. The breast with *Kannagi's* scent is lobbed at their
faces, and your uterus, an umbrella, opens out to shield the rain.
Albatross. You feel its ancient weight between breasts and legs.
Nose cut off, turned to stone, following him into the fire, because that
was always your designated place. A city's neck grows heavier, as
you writhe on an empty road, intestines uncoiled like Rapunzel's
hair, willing someone to grab hold. Intubated, medicated, oper-
ated on—once they find you, they outsource you, each breath
more precious than gold. *'Braveheart! Lightening! Fearless One!'*
News anchors, politicians, protestors chant. The hospital clock

ticks like a metronome, inhale exhale, inhale exhale. And as they name and blame and pray, you slip out quietly from the day. Stardust now, getting used to deep space, you zig, zag and zoom from place to place. A star is a star is a star is a star. Is what you are. An albatross in the Milky Way, soaring in a figure eight, that some would call infinity. *

Hiraeth– (Welsh) Homesickness for a home to which you cannot return, a home that never was. Homesickness tinged with grief or sadness over the lost or departed.

Nirbhaya (Fearless one in Hindi), was the name given to physiotherapist Jyoti Singh, 22, who was beaten and gang-raped in New Delhi, India, in December 2012, after boarding a bus. She succumbed to her injuries and died thirteen days after the incident, creating furor and outrage across the nation.

Kannagi: The central character of the Tamil epic Silapathikaram (100-300 CE), who took revenge on the King of Madurai, for wrongly imposing the death penalty on her husband Kovalan, by lobbing off her breast in anger, while cursing the city, inciting its destruction.

---

* *"Hiraeth" was first published in Anthology of Contemporary Poetry II Ed. Menaka Shivdasini. 2015 https://bigbridge.org/BB18/poetry/indianpoetryanthology/indian-poetry-anthology-contents.html*

KAVITA EZEKIEL MENDONCA

KNOTS

The story started with "Once upon a time"
Expected to end with "Happily ever after".
The Fairy Tales I read as a child
Promised such an ending
Art should imitate life.

Like monkeys in a barred cage
We kept vigil all that dark night
Then fell asleep one by one
Like koalas drunk on eucalyptus leaves
We fell exhausted on the bed.
The stars grew weary, the moon hid behind a cloud
Only she remained awake till morning light
the grass wet with dew, the sun still shy.

He never came home, never returned
The colored glass pieces in the kaleidoscope
No longer made meaningful patterns
I became Humpty Dumpty whom
'All the king's horses and all the king's men'
Could not put back together.

I want to be *Kintsugi*
Lacquer dusted with powdered gold, silver or platinum.
I want to untie the knots in my stomach
Play jump rope as in childhood days.
Before he left
My hair tossing in the wind
Carefree.

I want to be Kintsugi
Broken but fixable
I want the light
To come in through the cracks.

MARY ANNE MOHANRAJ

I LET GO HER HAND, DELIBERATELY

The rules were different when I was a child.
My parents feared the cost, a daughter's pain;
and if she strayed from old Sri Lankan rules,
she might be branded loose, or even wild.

I slept with boys and girls, or both, or more;
Monogamy was never meant for me.
The final fight—my little sister's plea—
barely enough to counter Amma's "whore!"

Years passed, the thread grew thin, but then
I had a child. Drawn back into familial embrace.
We hadn't married first, so *bastard* named—

—a word that had no weight for us. But when
our girl would reckless run at her own pace—
Amma, I understand your fear. We are the same.

PERVASIVE

Someone has hurt my child. I drown in grief;
worse than any pain I've felt, an ache
that settles in my bones; if I could only take
it for my own—but no. She is a trembling leaf

upon the wind, must learn herself to bear
the pounding of the storm. I stretch my arm
to wrap around, to shelter her from harm,
but all I give her now is helpless care.

I would have spared her this! Some pain
a parent must inflict: the immunizing shot,
the splinter's digging out, the walk away

from tearful child at school. That hurt will wane
and leave them strength. I fear this pain may not.
Inevitable woman's lot? *That* I will not say.

MAHVASH K. MOHTADULLAH

RAVAGED

It is my wedding day today; I am 17 years old
It is also the 6th anniversary of the 28th time "It" happened
And the 3rd anniversary of the 153rd time
I have this terrible memory—my teachers call it a photo-
graphic memory
I remember everything. I can't forget even when I want to
My mind is a notebook, each page blazing with the clarity of
vulgar recall
I have tried to be good, to remember only what I should
But I have this terrible memory...

Today I'm to wed my uncle—My father's cousin
For him, it is also the 6th anniversary of the 28th time "It"
happened
And all the anniversaries in between
I wonder if he remembers the 28th time... the 10th time....
The First time...
I wonder if his memory is as unforgiving as mine
My notebook has no entries on conjectures, or pain or anguish
Not mine, not anyone else's
It is only the sum total of the number of times "It" happened
Each page pristine, detailed, crystal clear, with edges as sharp
as knives
Bestowing countless paper cuts as they stir secretly in my
head
Those blessed paper cuts ... mental cuts .... numberless abra-
sions, innumerably inflicted to forget a page
To forget one instance.
That never happens.

But I find some peace as the physical pain temporarily cloaks me in its tenderly piercing grasp

Today I will become the wife of Harris lala* .... Harris....
No, I can't bring myself to drop the suffix
Maybe he will finally become nameless
Tranquilizingly, numbingly, mercifully nameless
My mother is relieved... she has been a silent witness (his co-conspirator?) to the last five anniversaries of when "It" first happened
My father hasn't really spoken to me in three years (his Protector?) .... not since the day I tried to tell him that his cousin ... his brother has ... has been ...
My mind still refuses to name "It"
Today I also learned that I'd stood first in the Board matriculation exam
I resent that accolade, that worldly consummation of my terrible memory
My terrifyingly acute, my savage, unrelenting memory

Today, my tormenter (my violator?) will become my partner for life
Today, I'm going to finally close the Notebook in my mind
Today, I'm going to be respectable once again
Today will be the First day of the consummation of my marriage
(Today will be the 389th time that I will be ravaged).

* *Lala*: a term of respect for an older man/brother.

CALLS TO PRIYA

The calls don't last long. Priya tells me. Hasty, and in haste, in waste of their common birth or relational worth. Words intrude, appear crude, suppose like crude oil or an intruder. Or pinch like eyes not washed for long. Or prick like minuscule splinters stuck in the sole of feet. The tone is exceedingly loud at times like a shrill drill digging in concrete. At times, like the sonic boom, zoom of fighter jets. Their words make her feel guilty for just breathing or saying they are hurting her. Disturbing her peace. They are being selfish. They, they speak meaner, shriekier. They, they splutter words like muddy, pungent water from a clogged drainpipe. Priya's beats pound, pound, pound like fists on an empty, gloomy drum, and her beats palpitate quick, quick, quicker like an old LP needle stuck without luck at the wrong speed. The trauma is real for her, constructed and deconstructed, repeatedly by them for her. Like a house burnt and rebuilt and burnt and rebuilt and burnt and rebuilt. Endless. Stuck in a matrixed time loop. Even Star Trek was able to find its way out. Not her. Not them. They blame her for not being good. She asks if they were ever good to her? "Shut up, shut up and shut up," is all they howl back and the winds from the oceans across echo. No amount of time and distance matter. Don't matter. Don't matter as new technologies are misused to multiply their meanness. Relatives.

SHELLY NAZ

SEPARATION

Translated from the Bengali by Kamrul Hassan

Today my parting-drenched stone that was lying in water
Is fickle in rain, her abysmal swimming
Played the tune of *Pakhwaaj** breaking the water-folds at noon.

The rain came in torrent; my mind received its first drop
shuddering
The doubt has been soaked; summer-ocean has sucked it wholly
After waiting muddy soil is filled with solid new gems, mica
and minerals

The potter created the mud-smelling me in his magical fingers
And set afresh new almond-shaped eyes, nose, face, lips
And alas he forgot to put the life inside.

I was not bad in fever and infirmity, disarrayed by lack of love
Half union has filled half separation
Tell me to whom should I go with the remaining half, a
scorched heart?

---

* Pakhwaaj: a musical instrument used in Indian classical music

MUSEUM

Translated from Bengali by Kamrul Hassan

The males are visitors, females mysterious museums
The closed golden gate will open only by love-ticket
The river entrapped inside her body will sing *ghazal*, the soaked tone
Will wipe the smut. Will come closer unconditionally

The magic of entering the museum, digging her trench
The males know lip-deep. They know archaeology, script of mind
Unwrapping the mystery. The intense mind hurries
The way fountain sprouts, the cork opens in wine glass

As if women are ancient *Harappa* or *Mohenjo-Daro*
You dig and unfurl history, the desperate folds
Filled with antiquities, you may find more *terracotta* inside
A stair smeared with sandalwood. The desired wine of addiction

As if a *Khajuraho* woman chockful with date juice
    You are also a traveler. The museum is wrapped by *saree*.

SOPHIA NAZ

COORDINATES

A crepuscular tourniquet
at sky-throat slowly turning
knob of blue to indigo
a body
is where latitude
of distance meets
longitude of memory

Over these coordinates you
layer lipstick, blush, eyeliner
earrings, scarf, shoes
and keep on walking.

MONA LISA POSTCARD

The rain went missing. Only canned laughter
opined by yawning firstborn of summer lawns
tinned millions of minions, droves of drones
that took and took their tithes and these
daily maws of man and beast you tried
to fend off or feed with manna descended
from heavens of once-hennaed hands

Fine fluid that could fill any china except
your own country, dark continent endless
spoonsful of sugar could not sweeten
tea leaves dried to stains.
Omens remained unread.

The salt on your face leaving
only faint navigations for the lost at sea
to decipher true north among the crossed
nuptial stars buried in folds of cloth
embroidered graves, yards where you had played,
girl who would be bird, now brood

Ma, from your lungs the heirlooms would shimmer
then disappear, keys to the honeyed forest
of *raga and ragini* grew scabs of rust,
locked up your hair, your leaping legs
shuffled, muffled in salwar webs.

Adjusting the pallu so no one would see
the bottomless well, a jigsaw puzzle
no matter how hard you tried to cue
the Mona Lisa postcard, her smile
was a vanished magic.
Just like you.

SUNAYNA PAL

BE LONGING.

Americans tell me
this isn't my home
I was born 8000 miles away
and had no right to move
to a place *they* came to first.

Indians tell me
it isn't my home
anymore.
I don't stay
or help her grow.

My kid calls me Indian.
My mom calls me American.
My friends call me Desi.
My colleagues call me Immigrant.
Who am I?

SWATI PAL

A WISH

I watched
The television
Dishing out
Kargil war
And Bollywood,
Khichdi news,
Real /fake
Bland/masala
All one.

I heard
The surgeon
Despair aloud
"What face
To operate?"
The mother
Begged him,
"Do something".

I felt
Eyes sting,
Pregnant widows
Stooping parents,
Cradle bodies
Cold, inert,
Who was
More dead?

I watched
I heard

I felt,
Another war
Simmered within
My soul,
No help
For either.

War breaches
All borders,
Wish peace
Would cross
Barbed wire
And mud
Equally effortlessly
And rule.

SUCHITA PARIKH-MUNDUL

ANTHEM

When trees bloom, they emit a collective scream
in sunlight. Their spring shrieks and petalled hysteria
confirm they don't grow garden-variety flowers.

Their blossoms are symptoms of madness,
of wildness rooted in lacerated tongues
that have seen more than revealed,

that fill your sky with revolution.
This unfolding isn't a hallucination,
it's an anthem. Listen.

KITCHEN SINK

Wipe hands of remnants of liquid emotion. Allow excess to drip into sink. Watch window become channel to external sphere. Listen to invisible howl that pervades air, circulated by fan blades in summer, monsoon, faux winter. Witness dreams enter kitchen, float overhead, threaten to burst. Watch fireflies swarm against norm in enclosed space of four walls and cracked ceiling. Accept introduction of fairy tale and brokerage of myth that is then lost and mourned. Turn on faucet, drown hands along with senses. Allow flood to wash away outdoors. Repeat.

SONALI PATTNAIK

SAY [9]

speak woman speak
howl whisper shriek
but say what you must say
your tongue your only tool
it's all they left behind
when they finished cutting through
your tongue your only tool
for sieving light from darkness
your words the darkest hour
before dawn harkens,
your words the ink
whose strokes will turn
the foggy screens of fear
into a tabula rasa
upon which the alphabets
of your truth align
all else they grey
all else is grey
till you say
that which only you
can say

AYESHA PERVEEN

BELT

Yes! I was head over heels in love
Felt like buying a gift for him
Was done with perfumes, clothes and wallets
Already, so thought of buying a top brand
Belt. Signature brown with a sophisticated frame
And tip, both embellished with high quality metal

Was excited to see him … to see his reaction about
The gift. He liked it, sober as he was, exacting his type
The leather as soft as he was and the frame standing out
Just like him, a successful entrepreneur with best qualification…
There was a tide in the relationship, till we got married.

Heaven were the early days and blessed were we….
Until… he seemed bored with me
The boredom overflowed turned into aggression
Verbal initially, till, one fine morning, when he
Not sober, trespassed the argument boundary!!!

The shouting, the belting was all I recalled when I got up
My soft skin bruised, aching as if shrieks coming from
Unidentifiable places. Dizzy, I got up from the ground and
Stumbled—something wrapped my feet. I made myself
Stable, bowed down to see what it was. Awestruck!!!
I saw the belt that I gifted him in the good old days…

NISHI PULUGURTHA

THE EMPTY HOUSE

I want to go home
to my mother
Ma—I call her
there is silence all around
I look for her
in the empty house.
I pick up a flower
a white flower that looks so nice
small white soft petals
like my ma's touch.
the green leaves
all around—colour
I knew I was looking for something
I do not know what
they say I forget things
maybe I do
I don't know.

TOO MANY QUESTIONS

What did you eat? Do you remember?
The voice asks me this.
I look at the face in front of me
I did not eat anything, I say
No, you did, the voice says
I look at the voice
I do not like it
I go into my room and lie on the bed
A big man stares at me
I smile
I get up, look at him and then walk back

Do you remember what you ate?
Bhaat, dal—I say and smile
And what else?
Lots of things, I say
No, no tell me correctly, the voice says
I do not like the voice.
Why is he asking me so many questions?

BASUDHARA ROY

THERAPY

Beckoned by the chromatic chronicle of this opal
its smooth edges spreading outwards like silk-maned waves,
I am now suddenly into it
and its rose-tinged grey gurgles on drowsy brown sands
three girls holding hands at sunset
as they splash water from a tin bucket in a cemented courtyard,
their bodies tender as new-sprouted basil leaves.

The scent of mango blossoms fills the air outside,
replaced immediately as one enters the house
with the smell of ripe bananas, rising chapattis and boiling milk.
The conch blows thrice and they gather to bow their heads at
the altar,
overcome less by devotion
than the glittering promise of stories they will tell each other
long into the dark—of hopes, dreams, desires, fears.

Suddenly the talons of the dusk are stronger
and there are night-winged insects everywhere.
Inside their brazen fluttering wings
she is eleven and claustrophobic,
her heart tactlessly pinned to her throat.
The room is bathed dark in the indigo light of the television screen
that shows the scoreboard of the second ODI between India
and Pakistan.

Most of the neighborhood is there.
Around fifteen of them—fathers, brothers, and three little
girls
are beating the undulating load-shedding of the city
with the zeal of a hired Exide battery,

the buoyant Wills and Sahara banners at Karachi firing their
hearts.
Uncle pulls her on his lap remarking how notorious she was at five.
She basks in his affection, her father smiling indulgently less
than five feet away.

On the screen the batsman hits a six and in the ecstatic uproar
something solid rises firmly against her hips.
She is not sure what it is and when she slightly shifts,
determined arms deftly pull her back upon it.
There is hot breath cascading down her neck
and the lap she is forced to sit on now
has become a blazing, ominous rock.

The hands stroking her knees have ranged under her frock
to rub with rough, thick fingers the insides of her thighs
and as they roam yet upwards
the mountain against her growing more desperate by the second,
her voice plunges down her throat like a pendant into a well.
Her mouth filled with nails she finally struggles to break free
and runs away,
blurting to the group that mother must be calling for dinner.

She never watches another cricket match
and the uncle doesn't flinch from offering benevolent attention
when forced to briefly meet on roofs, stairs, corridors.
She is not sure if loss clings to her because it has no language of
its own
or if she could not give it away being too naive to know its tongue.
But that room certainly fractured knowledge
forever into two halves.

Ever since, all that she heard and felt
have been two different colors
like hope and death,
like soil and sky,
like youth and age,
incapable of co-existing except in the heart's tight kernel
as a decrepit, weathered grey.

SUMANA ROY

SANDAKPHU

We wait to see the peak
as if it were a cake waiting to rise.
We check every few minutes
—time is in our legs, we count in steps—
for a fleck of white to pinch the frame.
It's the opposite of kohl bleeding from eyelids—
a smudge would be enough.

We think mountain-time as malleable as meat—
we think waiting can marinate everything.
The mountains are inexperienced—
their stones haven't learnt promptness of service.
We are impatient, as we are with the dead.
We complain, though we're unsure of our grief—
as if our presence was a question
for which the mountains have refused an answer.
We take it personally, as we do our destinies
and baldness patterns that run in families.
All tourists before and after us are competitors—
we compare merit, why Sandakphu should've swum
in their eyes and not ours,
the jealousy one feels for Sophocles,
why Aristotle should've written about him,
and not been our contemporary.
We don't know why we want to see the icy peaks,
their sun-specked aloneness, like art on a canvas,
cursed with a sail-less life, of only being watched.

We don't know how it'll change us, or even the world.
We only want a glimpse, and denied it,
we walk back to our minced life,
unforgiving but somehow innocent,
like a balloon that's leaked air,
whose body wasn't born for eternity.

KANCHENJUNGA

My eyes are cloudier than the day,
cloudier than time, than disease.
In my throat the mountains,
and their requests to move.
Sadness lays eggs easily—
its reproductive cycle like an insect's.

I wipe my eyes again,
as if these tears were blankets
I was folding for a future season.

In front of me are backs of heads,
as if the Kanchenjunga were a painting,
and Batasia Loop a museum.
Over their heads I expect to see it,
like a letterhead,
but it's not there.

My body's absorbed my heart like blotting paper.
I crouch in pain, I'm about to burst—
as if I were a pipe whose water's solidified.
Sadness feels like that—
hard; a hardening of what once was soft,
liquid and delightful, like love, or bread.

The Kanchenjunga doesn't appear.
There's disappointment.
It's as if the mountain hasn't kept an appointment.
Umbrellas open like rusty guns—
they carry the crowd like boats,
and soon, as the rain grows fluent,
ant-like drops stab the skin,
like ambulances without adjectives.

Wet, like a request, I sit by a culvert.
I wait, like a utensil,
collecting water that has no use.
This, too, will harden inside me,
like the icy peaks of Kanchenjunga—
sadness always finds its tourists. *

* *"Kanchenjunga", was previously published in* The Charles River Journal,
31 March 2020

SHRUTI SAREEN

JOBLESSNESS / UNEMPLOYMENT / BEROZGAARI

I sit, twiddling my fingers
wringing my hands,
my hands idle in my lap, no,
my hands slapping my forehead,
my hands raised in horror
my brain disintegrating
crumbling into depression.
When the desperation is so much
and the situation so bleak,
it makes you suicidal every day.
These hands and this brain
which could be doing so much
there's the pity and tragedy of it
wasting themselves away, becoming
senile at the age of 38 Yes, I am 38,
and i have a PhD in literature,
and i am jobless. And this situation
is becoming a crisis. And every
monotonous day fades into nothingness
when it could be so enlivening, so exciting.
But no, this country doesn't give a damn
about its people, but only the gold
and silver piling up in their coffers.
Privatising education, to keep it
solely in the hands of the rich.
Anyway, they want to kill the humanities,
beat them out. So why should they give us jobs?
It makes no sense, don't you see.

Better to keep our noses to the grind
keep us gasping for breath, begging
for a tiny part time job. As a chowkidar,
a gatekeeper, I would have earned more,
with better job security. The humanities
make you question, make you think,
make you doubt, make you protest,
make you alive with the spirit
of fire and change, ready to topple over
edifices. So, they need to be stamped out,
the fire turned to ash. Education,
should only be by the rich and for the rich
and it should only teach you commerce,
medicine, and engineering,
but never how to get manual scavengers
out of those damned drains.
So, the majority keep getting poorer
and poorer, living in strife, anxiety, depression,
mental trauma, while the billionaires
make it to the world list. This
ridiculous, uncivilised system
makes no sense. I often tell
my fellow job hunters
to stage mass suicide,
I live in India.

ASHA SEN

NOBODY LOVES A WIDOW

"how dare you dream you could stop loving someone just because they stopped living" (Bruce Dethlefsen).

Nobody loves a widow
In India, they burn them
But there are other ways
Sometimes a lover's jealousy
Brought on by a living memory
Of a love long dead
Lights up in fury
Turning everything to ashes once again

WORDS

I'm drowning in words
Your words, his words, her words
When will I find my words?
And will they ever be mine.

Caught in the texture of your thoughts
In the rhythms of your brain
I rest content
A happy captive

SHAFINUR SHAFIN

MY BODY, MY ENEMY

As a child, my mother warned me,
"Don't go outside, a ghost might eat you"
but mom, god will save me.
You always say god never let
any harm to children because they are
his favorite angel!
Mom had no answer!

When I grew up as a girl,
mom said, "Don't go outside alone!
There is always a vulture to snatch
and fly you away! You will never find mom again!"
but mom God will save me, right?
He doesn't like to separate me from you

When I became a teenager,
mom said, "it's always bad guys
if find you alone
they will prey on your body"

Now grown,
Still, I can't go alone in the dark.
Mom doesn't say anything.
It's me who is afraid.

I cannot help but feel,
That my body is a burden, a seal,
Keeping me chained, afraid to roam,
For fear of the eyes of society
now I understand,
there is No-God to save me
he is helpless too like mom

AYESHA

Her wisdom was sharper than ray
With her playmate horse and soulmate sword
She learned playing a perfect Orchestra
But perfect music can't be played forever
Can't be heard by all
It creates a fear
Fear to stand with its pierced beauty

Her curly head created that beautiful fear
No one was ready to hear, to face
That rebellious beauty...

PURVI SHAH

ON SAKSHI MALIK WRESTLING
A BRONZE AT RIO 2016

"Her bronze medal is a major victory over sexism in one of India's most conservative states, Haryana, where women have long been treated as second-class citizens and 'honour killings' and sex-selective abortions are rife." —Times of India, *June 23, 2017*

Where the men

    import brides to have some-
one to marry, where

the marriage

    bed is often a one-
way slaughterhouse, where

    generations of girls live
as ghosts in the river, we all

truly won
    gold

for first

wrestling
our way

    out
of a mother's

womb.

ON DIPA KARMAKAR SCORING FOURTH ON VAULT AT RIO 2016

Dipa, you are in excellent
company: the Olympics

are also fourth in worldwide
collaboration—to be first, you

would have had to be a world
        war, cluster bomb sprung

from the mouths
of those coalitions

of the willing.

DADOMA SHERPA

TREMOR

Only one thing comes in my mind whenever I hear of earthquake
Do you also think the same?
Bhaisakh 12 ?
Yes Bhaisakh 12?
Unexpected, Unwanted & unpredicted
Several homes fell, leaving several people homeless but mine
But my whole life was scattered
Severe earthquake was very devastating
My brother who just returned to home after enrolling into a
school
Who planned to end our poverty through the education
Who wanted to buy our mother a new sari and give our hard-
working father a retirement,
But future held something else for him.
Even our pets are beloved to us
However, this was my sibling, with whom I had grown up
felt as though I had fallen from the highest point
When my brother's body was pulled out from a destroyed house
After two hours of being lost
My innocent childhood could not distinguish
Whether it was reality or act of my brother who used to joke
around a lot
It did not take long for joy to turn to dread
Father's aid for elderly was crumbled within few times
Government relief fund could not bring back the son to his mother
I realized the true value of life after we moved out of my birth place
Leaving everything behind just for survival
We moved to the capital; dream city for everyone
Have you ever imagined?
How was a family of seven going to live in the unnamed city?
The more death toll increased, the faster my pulse beat

I can remember hearing rumors of rape and human trafficking cases
My mother always advised me to avoid engaging strangers, to
keep my mouth shut, and to decline their offers.
I was terrified of not only darkness but also of humans now
This is the reason
maybe the cause of my ongoing discomfort around strangers
Does the earthquake only affect Earth?
Unfortunately, the entire house, family, and existence
Aftershocks and catastrophes remind me of you, my brother
Discovered lines written with tears and blood
today when I flip through old books
And others were unable to even open.

FARAH SIDDIQUI

I CAN BREATHE

I can breathe

Heavy heart
Stuffed lungs
My body don't give up
On me

Be it violence
Like the foot on
George Floyd's neck
Suffocating
The breath
From coming
Till finally
He could not take it
Anymore
I wish he threw the
Foot back on
The racist face

Be it cancer
That falls in love
With my brother
Makes him suffer
With agony
Of tight jaw
And skin eruptions
Heavy tongue
Stifled voice
I cannot wait

To throw the cancer cells
Miles away from his body
Let him breathe

Be it Covid 19
That will try to enter through the
Windpipe
And dance in the lung
Trying to stop my breath
You cannot win
Against my body
And my soul
No matter who you are.
Disease of Racism
Cancer cells
Or Virus
You won't win
I will breathe.

JASPAL KAUR SINGH

REFUGEE: DELHI DAYS
AS A STATELESS CITIZEN

I.

waiting in long queues
at foreign registration office
dust of New Delhi buses
in mouth, nostrils, lungs

    a camel in the desert
    & fly settles in mouth
    hungry hands grab
    tender mountain orchids

the sub-inspector of police
stares at my young body
his brusque voice enters
my pores my mind my being

    crush of teeth snaps fly
    tiny wings lodge in throat
    iced water for 5 paisa
    at Lady Hardinge bus stop

fearful of being denied extension
to live and learn in ancestral home
& see emerald fields with golden grainstalks
as re-remembered by grandmother in Burma

       In distant land, a borrowed home
       wrested from slumbering breasts
       we required certificate of identity
       our travel documents to escape

refugees from our birthland
labelled and othered as illegitimate
"returned" to India as overseas *musafir*
from desolate land, unlike poor Zafar

       without solace, without love
       we became refugees for years
       harassed annually & made to wait
       hours upon hours after school

my nineteen-year-old self
rigid with fear and defiance
my Indianness a costume
in long braid & white salwar kameez

       red stone building stares
       at my face with belligerence
       yellow walls sneer at our quest
       descendants of Partition Punjabi

              President's Estate royal buildings reject
              my shabby appearance on its pristine lanes
              as if gum stuck to red leather shoesoles
              soulless, deadened, excessive, ravenous

II.

one summer i was one day late
to renew the certificate of identity
his eyes stonecold and icy,
lips surly, the sub inspector said—

> *bring cold cash or you will be jailed*
> *your permit expired, you are refugees now*
> *without rights, without home, without country*
> *straddling borders, you are now itinerant*

Malini and I, college mates
sat outside on stony bench
easy target for many men
she   a Delhi girl   told me

about Tihar, the dreaded jail
women raped & tortured by police
my relatives had no money for the fine
I waited for the DSP until evening

fear rising to the arid blue sky
that provided no mercy or reprieve
fear rising to the pipul tree
raucous crows laughing and jeering

then, he came, the sub-inspector:

> *you are lucky, he will see you*
> *but no guarantees that*
> *you will not be fined or jailed*

our lives in formless Delhi
where the Immigration Officer—
his stare quizzical, his full lips
parting in small triumphant smile

dark hair parted in middle—
said: *You are a smart and educated*
Delhi girl, why are you late, hmmm?
I'm signing your documents

this one time, but remember
next time, you will not be so lucky
you could be jailed or deported
what then? he rested his hand

on my arm shoulders
his dark eyes on my lips.

III.

Parents, refused travel documents,
& stuck back in soulless birthplace,
messaged: *stay with Delhi
relatives & go to school*

*you are given a chance
to live a life of freedom
you are given a chance
to redream and rewrite*

—*away* from Ne Win's army
and their stenguns   their stenguns
—*away* from xenophobia and   violence
        unleashed by the   government

—*away* from the Bureau of Special Investigation
    outside our home   frisking us daily for   contraband
—*away* from hunger, from reeducation camps, from slogans
        death, devastation   rape and murder

IV.

for four more years I went
with gifts of a parker pen
a length of terylene
some sweets and a watch

to grease the palms
of the sub inspector
my lipstick red, cheeks pink
short sleeveless black dress

slight highheels and a red purse
so that, even when on time,
fear of being deported
like a bad refugee

back to the land of my birth
so that he will sign
so that he will smile
so that he will make me legitimate

in the lands of my ancestors
my exotic modern Indianness my badge
my Jasmine perfume my signature—
legitimize me, so I can have a home.

MEMORIES OF HOMES AND NESTS

partition stole my grandparents
& my elder sister's Punjab birthplace
split like bark on neem trees
bitterness and husk our legacy

midnight treks and ghost trains
looted home and lost land
torn dupattas and stained clothes
jagged nails and dispersed limbs

violence on bodies and legitimacies
disappearing in communal clashes
my parents returned to birthplace
of Burma, years of trips to borders

of Thailand and China for goods
to trade in Taunggyi, my home—
I was born in sonborn hospital
unlucky third daughter

grandma sulked and shamed Ma,
called her low caste woman
from a tailoring Sikh community
even though casteless, we discriminate

as if all of us are supposed to be
bees in a hive sweet as honey
our gurudwaras became eyesores
for Burmans, who called us

black foreigners, the *kula mai*
smell of *ghee* and *dahi* our signature
at school, my brother's red turban yanked
from long hair, taunted and laughed at

after the military coup of '62

my father's shop confiscated
daylight robbery by General Ne Win
led to resistance by many of all races,
then students' bodies buried in shallow graves
we left home, penniless, dreamless,
to return "home", to our never seen
ancestral land and our people

there, in New Delhi, we were identified
as imported, haunted by stares
as if butterflies pinned to a board
by a zoologist who simply accumulated

colorful wings and bright dust
for visitors of exotic things
we fluttered and twisted our limbs
ghosts in ancient ancestral home

New Delhi: you enveloped us—
                    a city of dreams
                    a city of demons
                    a city for descendants
                    a city of hot nights
                    a city of violence
                    a city of rejections

yet: a city that loved—
                    a city that nurtured
                    a city that touched
                    softy on cool nights
                    starry and filled
                    with moonlit junebugs
                    a city of lakes and gardens
                    a city of temples and gurudwaras
                    a city of ancient forts and palaces

burning ghats on Jamuna
ring road encircling
old and new Delhi
like an old crone

with long brown arms
and long white hair
and I, even though stateless
longing to belong, felt land shift

below diasporic peripatetic feet
I felt my self-wandering again
unable to find space or solace
to nest, like the koel

using mimicry to belong
or, like the ani, building
communal homes for descendants
in the land of my ancestors.

KALPNA SINGH-CHITNIS

IS ANYONE LISTENING?

She has lost her mind. It's impossible to care for her.
A WhatsApp message notifies in the middle of the night.
I promise not to talk about the messenger.

They are considering a mental asylum or a senior home.
They are waiting for her lab results and the doctor's note.
She no longer has a say.

She can't remember her whereabouts, sits half-naked all day.
She can no longer button her blouse,
clean herself. She is a mess.

She can't stand on her own, can't walk a little distance.
She refuses her cane and hopes. She is convinced,
it's time for her to go now.

Her hands—like branches of a desiccating tree
birds have abandoned. Her hollow bones sing all night
the lullaby her mother sang to her. But she can't sleep.

She can't remember the days of the week,
the number of years she has lived. Do you?
Do the math...

Add her age with the ages of all her children and grandchildren.
She lives in their flesh, blood, and bone marrow. Let's not forget,
she is just living on another plane where we have yet to arrive.

She can't keep track of time, doesn't know if it's day or night
and keeps calling. Cut the crap! Send her to a madhouse!
Shut the noises she makes—just a bit of advice.

It's a lockdown, and she wants to go elsewhere.
Where, she doesn't know. Millions have lost their jobs,
and she has lost her mind! Millions have died, but she is still
living.

It's easier said than done.
You privileged ones, sitting afar,
you are only eligible to foot her bills and be entertained.

People are dying of hunger, and she is wasteful,
smears her food all over her body and face, worse than a child.
She soiled the elevator the other day. How embarrassing!

She needs a diaper change every two hours.
Go away, you perfect mess! Stop knocking!
People are working from home, don't you know?

They have bills to pay, family to care for.
But she keeps coming and coming,
knocking and knocking,

until a door opens, and she feels a blow on her face,
punch after punch on her forehead, until she collapses,
choking on her children's names, and goes silent

SERMON

If I die of an assault,
do not file a report.
It isn't the first time.

Do not go to a court
seeking justice.
There is none.

Do not allow politicians to enter
my village and town.
No media, no clowns.

No debauchery of whataboutery.
Do not bother hanging my perpetrators,
they will be born again in a multitude.

Do not imprison them,
they can't be restrained.
I'll be violated again, just in another place and time.

If you hope to do anything for change,
write an epic or a tale in my name,
and teach it if you can, in every school on earth.

If you are a woman, tell my story to your sons.
If you are a man, tell it to your daughters.
If you are a preacher, teach it as a sermon to the believers.

KASHIANA SINGH

TO DELIVER ANOTHER WOMAN

let us assume an age for the sake of argument
let us go with 13 since girls become women around then
coming of age begins with instructions that she should wear
double panties
and sanitary pads, ensure that the boxed pleats of her grey
cambric skirt don't stain
her kajal streaked eyes are meant to look down, prohibited
slant glances
she is sshhh'ed into corners of rooms, sits in stoic silence, a
lamb before the butcher's knife
her folded legs tight locked inside home-made quilts, a tent to
silence her rearing cries
like a punctured stencil she draws patterns on the carved bed
with her fists
she screams & screams, her chest throbbing into her mother's
softness
the truth is that a girl at 13 is not even woman
a lotus maybe sometimes a fungus which is also a flower
maybe a hydrangea bloom with seeds the size of cracked
peppercorns
a blazing red bud, a lidless, petal less bud, flush with fertility
craving the permission to swim shave or spool music
revolting by entering holy premises of the kitchen, guarded
pure
her acidic fingers fermenting pickles, drenched in a salmon
like scent
she thrives in plotting a future, of satiation, of relentless desire
she does not know that her ancestors will continue to be
estranged

they will surround her, like an opaque cyclone cloud and spit
at her
tehzeeb
spit at her inability to accept   taqdeer
she is now 50 and has a lotus growing inside her breast
she is now a flattened breast whose marrow has been sucked
her hands peel away the opaque cinnamon film on her lisping skin
she stares stares at the mirror on a scarred wall, her naked
breast diced
then she stares at her own face at 70 a dehydrated fig that
smirks inside her throat
an admonition crushed inside teeth calcified like salted edges
of an ocean
she chokes as she spews an endless curse
fading eyes drown in the luscious copper bowl
she stays like a spell beneath the untended feet of forgotten
deities
banished from the latched temple of her omen pocked body
she lets grief perch on her blackest tongue, curse of a trembling
moon
many women rise like a howl above banyan roots, many legged,
many armed
are they goddesses?
elsewhere a heavy winged bustard with a wing span as wide as
an ocean
spreads a shadow across the firmament
soaring tender & alive on the uglier side of a waning moon
an eclipse looming like a threat
screams rising like a malignant furnace
rousing from the bowels of an unrelenting earth
its mouth held open with forceps
with bloated flesh and belching mouths
multitudes of long haired daayans plunging their hands deep,
digging
into the waning debris
of chants, to deliver another woman
then holding a neck, till its tiny bones crack, crackle
a cackle rising from their collective throats, an orgasm of cymbals
stirring awake brigades of bats inside barren caves

INSTRUCTING A YOGA CLASS

Step outside this coquettish altar, a container
Lounge into yourself, lengthen long in spine
Ease your breath, let it unwind, in interludes
Let in every thought towards its navel center

You are gripping the sides of your own hide
Fingers clawing into the backs of your knees
Perhaps, you try to run the warmth of palms
Up and down your legs, torso in a balasana

Examine awkwardness of breath, it is a river
Imagine you are floating in the galaxy above
Allow every person in shavasna around you
To also rise, let them, become constellation

Find the craters, touch the hollows, gentle
Make space for the woman next to you too
Browse barefoot into the forest, soles wet
Follow the footprints of a mycorrhizal web

Then the instructor says, drop knees down
Allow this flesh to die, alone like when born
Swim beyond thoughts, float towards a ghat
Gasp as you arrive, a hush settling into tears *

* *"Instructing a Yoga Class" was first published in* Stone Poetry Quarterly *in May 2023*

SUKRITA

HOMELESS

The foetus in the sobbing womb
of the girl child is

an offspring of terror
of the skies:
thunder, lightning, hail storms
falling over her;

Of the knife rubbing
just a little deeper
on her throbbing throat

Her face a rock
Eyes turned into stones
A mother without a heart
Wanting to give birth

To defy death
And put men
in the docks

*

Rani left truth
back home with her mother
in her qasba,

With a mountain of lies on her
Thin shoulders
She arrived safe and sound,
Spilling some of it
To survive the journey
To this big city

Rani will live long
She carries her burden lightly

***

PARTING AGAIN

Sadness sits like
a snake in my belly
turning and twisting

Giving me hysterics

It sits
Hissing subtle threats
of yet another severance,

Emitting warnings
through my glassy
half-closed eyes
Forcing them open
to
stone stillness,
snow silence,
and a reptile alertness

Sadness travels down my spine
reaching my womb...

Your own home
where I held you tight
till you
pushed your way
into a world of

Self, identity and
Sadness

***

PRAMILA VENKATESWARAN

TWO STORIES[10]

I touch the smoothness of my belly:
it is still taut pregnant with
the knowing seed yet to gain form.
My expectation grows imperceptibly
in proportion with my heart
I fail to guard its rush.

No no no no no, I wail,
as crimson flares the water.

You can try again, relatives echo.

I touch the smooth skin of my belly:
it is tranquil
undisturbed by my cramps   my heart
a wrung sponge.

The body knows what it wants.
It hoards memories, it releases.

2

Hum do humaara do planted firmly in baba's brain,
he orders, *you have to get rid of it.*
Amma does not tell him she is already attached
to the unnamed growing fiercely
joining its desire with her yearning.

You had to get pregnant, didn't you?
His voice, a hard hand pushing her desire down,
unbirthing it.
The doctor's potion becomes his weapon.

But the doctor's poison defeats his wish.
A son is born to confront the father fleeing
from what is to be.

VIVIMARIE VANDERPOORTEN

GIRL, BEAUTIFUL.

They may say that beauty is only skin deep
But I was always taught
That for a girl to be pretty was pretty much
Everything.
Rhymes I learnt as a child
Were cited as evidence
"where are you going to my pretty maid"
"my face is my fortune, sir, she said"
So I carried the burden of needing to be beautiful
heavy on my back
for all of the years.
At sixteen, adolescent acne
scrawled across my face
the graffiti of growing up

my father, ever practical
mixed sandalwood powder and cold water
into a paste
and handed it to me while I was engaged with equations
and trigonometry
"I have no dowry to give your future husband,
so please apply this paste and stop touching
your face"
And so beauty turned from burden
into obedience
into submission
into a rule
into the only adjective that mattered.

So today when you told me
I was a beautiful person
And that I should only try to be healthy
It felt a lot like
laying down a load,
it sounded like
beauty had arisen from beneath the bones
where it hurt,
and settled comfortably
just a little under my skin.

CEASEFIRE

Before her hippocampus changed
my mother-in-law
had declared war on me
and drew the battle lines clear
There was a fort
between her kitchen
and mine
Reasons for rivalry
were lost in a murky complexity
of history and property
Her husband
and mine
were the failed peace-makers
For want of survival
as the years passed by
an uneasy truce
transpired
with only sporadic
grenades of
accusation hurled my way.

Now plaques and tangles
have invaded her brain
and the simplest of tasks
are a struggle for her.
Language, her former weapon
often evades her
and she searches for the
right words
as in a field full of landmines.
In the failed connections
between neurons
she sometimes smiles at me
as pure as an infant
as I help her get dressed.
In the mist of missing memories
and field of forgotten things
I exist—
and at an unspeakable price—
enemy
no more

PARROT

(Trincomalee, Sri Lanka, ten years after the end of the war)

The woman who
lost her son in the war
shows me his framed photograph.
But in his smile
there is no hint of wrists firing
a gun
nor the shadow of hands hurling
grenades.
In his clothes, no hint of a striped uniform.
Like the parrot she now keeps caged
and in whose wings she has clipped
there is no trace
of the possibility of flight.
But as the parrot hops around in his iron cage
you can see the memory of
freedom in his eyes
a home land,
branches and green fields
in his now non-existent wings

RASHNA WADIA

A HAIBUN: NAVAJO GIRL/INDIAN GIRL

Navajo sings rain
dance in earthen beat drum
to white men's ignorance

Dressed in three tiers of royal blue velvet spilling beneath the decorative concho of her waistline, a girl is branded—*Navajo*.

She stands like a bird in flight, brown wings carry her to ancestors under the loam, heartbeat strong. She smiles of herself; her brothers and sisters linked in circles, wrapped around safe folds of ceremonious *chant beat drum*.

The girl's eyes shut, and open to masala chai spices wrapped inside silk saris in shades of spilled blood draped over the small frame of smooth skin; the scent of moth-balls, pungent and familiar; she steps one foot at a time on fish chalked pavement; watches her mother bend forward to place the red dot between her brows, lay the garland of red roses around her neck, and kiss her.

A white boy of Columbus stands in procession and watches. He steps forward and motions to embrace the *Navajo* Girl, the *Indian* Girl.

She reaches for him, the one she hopes to call, *brother*. But he spits instead. His saliva, sour in the mouth of rancid words flies splat onto the face of the *Navajo* girl, the *Indian* Girl. Thick mucus sticks to jagged lines stretched silent across her forehead, and she wails as any girl would. Her tears turn to rain that floods the land that soaks the earth of her ancestors across an ocean to a country that births monsoons and men who pull oxen carts their feet caked black; drowning in mud. An *Indian* girl dreams

golden bangles jingling around her feet as she dances the scent of sandalwood on holy days, the incense of agarbatti mixed with the scent of wet earth, mixed with the jeers of white boys who pretend pow pow with toy guns and play tom toms for a brown girl who steps into America to the drumming of a tabla

Indians dance rain
parched voices of white men's hate
drenched in monsoon

MY NAME IS NOT NAVAJO

blue-eyed girls in floral pink
dresses and lace trim socks
giggled when I jumped
double dutch high over
ropes slapped down on
concrete circled in singsong
drum beats played on the
dirty mouths of white boys
1-2-3-4-5 you're out!
my black hair two braided
ropes tied tightly a noose for
the lynching of ancient beats
still beating under the loam
they stole, hungry for sweet
blood they spilled when
they pushed me down on a
playground their tongues
like whips on masala chai
fingers broken they branded
me the name *Navajo*
claimed my nose Indian
ski slope nose Navajo
claimed my legs Indian
hairy legs Navajo
but my name is not *Navajo.*
shut up ugly Navajo!
their laughter echoed
Columbus of empty desert
rock that held the hot coaled
slur planted inside my little
girl fists meant to punch
homegrown smirks off
white boys who become
their fathers in suits and see
me driving to yoga class on
the pretty side of town their
middle fingers erect
still calling me names not
my own.

SHERNAZ WADIA

BROKENNESS

The world is fractured...
inequality, despotism, injustices, violence,
war ravished cities, broken humanity
fenced behind the barbed wires of cruelty

past wounds sprout in poisoned minds
hatred polarises, fear asphyxiates,
there is turbulence under the heavens
the world is fractured...

let us question ourselves—why
the racism, conflict-ridden notions
mental walls that barricade love
and kindness, hope and faith

let us repair ourselves first
let us not despair; minds reposed,
reflective, purposeful, compassionate...
then begin to heal our fractured world

fix its lesions with the salve of tenderness
link hands in true togetherness
lift up hearts, embrace diversity
create a sanctuary of peace and harmony

NEED OF OUR UNCERTAIN TIMES

Loneliness grapples
with itself on social media
 I sense sleepless eyes
flecked with concern, stress, terror

hands reaching out for hugs
palms wanting warmth
make me stretch out mine
but I can't reach them.

in these uncertain times,
words rarely hold
the weight of their meaning
I sit in silence, sending out vibes
of love, light, hope and peace *

* *Both "Brokenness" and "Need of Our Uncertain Times" were published in https://
www.boloji.com/poem/27433/brokenness and the Facebook group* The Coeur in
Courage: Poetry, Awakening, Musings & More

S.I WELAGEDARA (SHEHANI)

THE POLITICS OF THE PINK CUPCAKE

Whipped-cream words and hugs of extra sugar
Blended and beaten
Until its silken smooth
—in other words, perfect, ideal, flawless—
Spread over rough edges
With a knife,
All buttered up: no messes, no marks.
Did I say flawless?
Dripping sweetness in lieu of
The blanks in black-white papers,
Compensating for the spaces in the wages.
One-day grand treat,
(Congratulations!
You survived another three-sixty-five days
Of wandering hands,
Dismissive nods,
And nominal round tables)
Another year, and counting
To finger-off the icing
To get to the spongy core.
And maybe, just maybe,
Bite into the frozen biases.

ATHER ZIA

DEMOLISHING HOMES IN KASHMIR

for we are driven insane
it is time to love insanely.
our broken homes
our broken bodies
our hearts glued from
a million pieces
insanely in love
now
tomorrow
forever

AFTER THE WAR

i wish you sleep well.
and wake again and again.
to search for me
after the war

i wish your bed is warm.
and cold in all spaces
where my body would be
after the war

i wish the moon is shining,
in your window pouring
silver runnels of light
till my eyes would drip on yours
after the war

i wish the birds are singing.
and quiet, not happy for
the distance that exists
between us,
after the war

i wish the sun rises
and sets on the ancient pattern
yet the days are longer than hours,
moving like a river of ice
after the war

i wish the streets decked like brides
wearing camouflage over their robes red
aren't bombed,
and the address stays
after the war

i wish
one day upon waking up

you hang the moon over the bed
quieten the birds,
pull curtains to keep the sun out
and return
to where i write this, that
and other reminders—
after the war

AFTER THE CRACKDOWN

after the crackdown
the women receive men
and their bodies black and blue
they pretend to unsee
the wounds that look
angrier than husbands

the women are brisk—
first, they bring cold water to drink
then they rub ointments into the welts
drawing warm baths
handing clean towels
they do not look up

the women make sure
dignity returns into cold homes
warm food and warm beds
after soldiers retreat—

in the dead of night
when sleep enters some beds
the women visit the attics
where the wooden chests are broken
earthen vats turned upside down
the ceiling pried open,
honeycomb oozing
mustard oil mixed with rice
chili mixed with powdered milk

after the crackdown
salvaging whatever they can
of men, and things
women, when done if ever
pray to find the darkest corner
to stitch their torn garments
as effortlessly with a tear
and a prayer, as their only companions

NOTES

1. 'Agrawal's "Yashodhara" reveals that while the entire world celebrates Buddha's enlightenment, few spare a thought for the feelings of his wife Yashodhara, whom he abandoned without a word along with their seven-day-old son, Rahul, one night. The poem seeks to put Yashodhara's disillusionment and pain into perspective. It seeks to look at the incident from the deserted woman's point of view.

2. 'Basu's "At the Border" was inspired by the 2018 zero-tolerance policy for undocumented asylum seekers at the US border, leading to children being separated from their parents. The shock of witnessing this on news media made her reflect on her own journey as an immigrant in the US.

3. Chakravarty's "Severed Tongue" refers to Khona (also known as Lilavati), a legendary Bengali woman astrologer and poet, is believed to have lived in the Rarh region (Southern Bengal), between the 9th and 12th centuries AD. According to some versions of the story, she learned astrology from her father-in-law Varahamihir, one of the nine jewels in the court of Emperor Chandragupta II or Vikramaditya. Her poetry, encapsulating her wisdom and clairvoyant powers in cryptic sayings called vachans, became famous across the region and beyond. According to legend, Khona aroused masculine ire and jealousy when she surpassed Varahamihir in the practice of astrology. She was persecuted by the male establishment. Ultimately this led to her tongue being cut off in an act of silencing. But her sayings survived and continue to be cherished and widely circulated in eastern India and Bangladesh even today. An earthen mound in Chandraketugarh, associated with the names of Khona

and Mihir, is popularly believed to contain the buried ruins of their lives.

4. Doshi was commissioned to write a poem in response to a piece of art by the Royal Academy of Arts Magazine, and she chose the Rajput miniature "Tiger-woman" that she had seen at the Yale University Art Gallery— "because there was something haunting and powerful about the painting". Here's a link to the painting: https://artgallery.yale.edu/collections/objects/30275

5. Gaur's poem refers to an incident where a 19-year-old Dalit girl was abducted and gang raped by four men in Uttar Pradesh's Hathras district on September 14, 2020, and she was subjected to brutal torture by breaking her bones and cutting off her tongue. She was hurriedly cremated without the presence of her traumatised family.

6. Ghosh's "Kafka's World" depicts the COVID-19 Pandemic with devastations all over the world, migrants walked miles on bare feet in India to reach their homes.

7. Iyer's poem was inspired by the Citizenship Amendment Act that was passed by the Indian government in 2019 and which gave only some religious minorities special privileges for Indian citizenship. The poem reflects the confusion and despair caused by the exclusion.

8. Limbu's poem is based on the real incident and about the experiences of a girl child who had witnessed the war between the former Nepalese royal government and the Communist Party (Maoist) during the People's War in Nepal between 1996 to 2006.

9. Pattnaik's poem is inspired by Urdu poet Faiz Ahmad Faiz's *bol* which urges us to speak the truth, no matter what little time we think we have, reminding us that it is enough to say what needs to be said.

10. Venkateswaran's poem is set in the context of Prime Minister Indira Gandhi's forced abortion policy that made men force their wives to abort their babies if they already had two children.

ABOUT THE EDITORS AND CONTRIBUTORS

EDITORS

Lopamudra Basu, Ph.D. is Professor of English at University of Wisconsin-Stout. She is the author of *Ayad Akhtar, the American Nation and its Others After 9/11: Homeland Insecurity* (Lexington Books, December, 2018) and the co-editor of *Passage to Manhattan: Critical Essays on Meena Alexander,* Cambridge Scholars Publishing, UK, 2009. Her current scholarly interests include trauma studies, post 9/11 American literature. and postcolonial poetry. Her poetry has been published in journals like *Journal of Commonwealth and Postcolonial Studies, Barstow and Grand, Dhaka Review, Postcolonial Text, Prachya Review, Silver Birch Press blog,* and in the anthologies *Modern English Poetry by Younger Indians* (Sahitya Akademi) and *Best Asian Poetry 2021-2022 (Kitaab), Yearbook of Indian Poetry in English 2022, and the Poetry Calendars of the Wisconsin Fellowship of Poets.* Her scholarly essays have been published in journals like *Humanities, Women's Studies Studies in the Novel, South Asian Review, Nebula, Journal of Commonwealth and Postcolonial Studies, Social Text,* and in the anthologies *Rites of Passage in Postcolonial Women's Writing* (Rodopi, 2010), *Drawing From Life: Memory and Subjectivity in Comic Art* (University of Mississippi Press, 2013), *Masks of Threat : South Asian Racialization and Belonging after 9/11* (Lexington 2016), *A History of Indian Poetry in English* (Cambridge University Press, 2016), and in *Narratives of Trauma in South Asian Literature(Routledge, 2023).* She is currently working on a book of poems on Covid to memorialize the many personal losses she encountered as well as to change the absence of Covid memoirs from India.

Feroza Jussawalla, Ph.D. is Professor Emerita at the University of New Mexico., where she won the Alumni Teaching Award in 2014. She taught at the University of Texas at El Paso from 1980-2001 and at the University of New Mexico from 2001-2021. She is the author and co-editor of several books, primarily on Postcolonial Literatures: *Family Quarrels: Towards a Criticism of Indian Writing in English*, (Peter Lang 1984), *Interviews with Writers of the Postcolonial World* (Mississippi 1997), *Conversations with V.S. Naipaul*, (Mississippi 1999), and *Emerging South Asian Women's Writing*, (Peter Lang 2017). Most recently she has co-edited, *Memory, Voice and Identity: Muslim Women's Writing from Across the Middle East* (Routledge 2020), and *Muslim Women's Writing, from South and South East Asia*, (Routledge 2023). Her most recent pedagogical article "Teaching the Cousinship of Experience: The Postcolonial Bildungsroman Across Time and Cultures" is collected in *Teaching South Asian Anglophone Diasporic Literature* edited by Nalini Iyer and Pallavi Rastogi (MLA 2024). She has thirty plus book chapters and articles, and several poems published separately. Her additional specialization is in D.H. Lawrence. Her collection of poems is *Chiffon Saris* 2003. Her poems for Silver Birch Press are "Still Waiting" (2021), "Wake Up" (2022), "Mother Ganga" (2022), "Elegy for My Trees" (2022), and "More Chile and Less Curry" (2023). She also has a poem titled "Taos Pueblo" (2021) published in Poetry and Places. Most recently, she published, "Hyder Park," a poem in honor of the park that helped her heal from breast cancer, in the *One Albuquerque* anthology, published by the UNM press, (2024).

CONTRIBUTORS

Vinita Agrawal's latest collection of poems *Twilight Language* (Indian edition: *The Natural Language of Grief*) was adjudged the winner of the Proverse Prize 2021. She is the author of five books of poetry: *Two Full Moons* (Bombaykala Books), *Words Not Spoken* (Brown Critique), *The Longest Pleasure* (Finishing Line Press) and *The Silk Of Hunger* (AuthorsPress),

She is based in Indore, India. She was awarded the Rabindranath Tagore Literary Prize 2018 and the Gayatri GaMarsh Memorial Award for Literary Excellence, USA, 2015. She has won the Proverse Poetry Prize 2017 and 2022 and the Hawkers Prize 2019. Her work was shortlisted for the inaugural Dipankar Khiwani Memorial Prize, 2021. Her poems have won first prize at Hour of Writes. She won the Wordweavers Poetry contest in 2014 and the first prize in the Architectural Poetry Competition, 3rd Cycle – Improvisation 2021. She is the Poetry Editor with *Usawa Literary Review*. Her poems have been published in *Mascara Literary Review, Human Obscura, The Global South, Amphibian, Fox Chase Review, Indian Quarterly, Asian Cha*, and *Punch Magazine* among others. She co-edits the Yearbook series of Indian Poetry in English (Hawakal) and has edited *Open Your Eyes: An Anthology on Climate Change* (Hawakal) and a memoir-anthology on the Kashmiri poet Ghulam Rasool Nazki (Ink Links). She is on the Advisory Board of the Tagore Literary Prize and on the Global Judging Panel of SheInsprawrds. She is on the Advisory Council of G100, India. You can find her work at www.vinitawords.com

Zaithoon Bin Ahamed is a content writer/editor and communications/PR specialist. She has played multiple roles across diverse industries, ranging from media, financial news reporting, investment research publishing services, marketing, corporate communications and PR. She loves travelling, experiencing new cultures and exotic cuisines, and enjoys yoga and meditation. She is currently the Head of Corporate Communications at WSO2, a US-based technology company. Zai is from Sri Lanka and lives in Colombo.

Usha Akella has authored nine books including musical dramas, poetry collections, and creative non-fiction narratives. She is the founder of Matwaala (www.matwaala.com) and hosts www.the-pov.com.

Dilruba Z. Ara is the author of two novels *A List of Offences* and *Blame*, and a collection of stories titled *Detached Belonging*. Translated into numerous languages, her writings have appeared in *Chattahoochee Review* (USA), *Drunken Boat* (USA), *Dragoman Journal of Translation Studies* (Belgium and the

UAE), *Vista* (Pakistan) *Asia Writes* (Singapore), *Democratic World Magazine and Kirtya* (India), *The Daily Star and Bangla Academy Journal* (Dhaka), Swedish Institute and *Shipwrights Review* (Sweden).

Shamim Azad is a bilingual author and one of the best-known Bengali poets in the UK. She has published books including collections of poems, plays, children's books, novels and translations. Azad received the Bangla Academy Literary Award in Poetry, the highest literary award in Bangladesh, and the National Lottery award in the United Kingdom.

Kanwalpreet, Ph.D., teaches Political Science to students in a college affiliated with Panjab University, Chandigarh, India. Writing is a passion for her. She has written 12 books and is working on a few more. She writes mainly fiction, and delves into literature for children. Her first book, *Looking Back with A Twinkle,* won accolades from Chandigarh Sahitya Akademi, a prestigious body that encourages writers. The Akademi gave her a grant for her next book, *Rings of Life,* a collection of 13 short stories whose protagonists are women. *A Magic Combo* is a collection of 31 poems and 13 short stories for children.

Pragya Bajpai, Ph.D., is a poet, artist, and mother of two, serving at the National Defence Academy, Ministry of Defence. She has authored two poetry collections: *A Potpourri of Proverbs* (2021) and *Conversations on Cue* (2022). She has also co-edited four anthologies celebrating the armed forces.

Alka Balain loves to paint and write. Her writings have appeared/will appear in online journals: *Usawa Literary Review,* kitaab.org, Indian Periodical, AlSphere, LiveWire, Poet mag, Women's Web, Readomania, Visual Verse, Brahmaand, *The Hooghly Review* and Dreich. She is presently club chair of the Writing Club of Indian Women's Association, Singapore. (on Instagram)

Laksmisree Banerjee, Ph.D. is a Senior Fulbright Scholar, Commonwealth Scholar and National Scholar from Calcutta University, a UGC Post-Doctoral Research Awardee and Former Vice Chancellor & Pro Vice Chancellor of Kolhan University, Eastern India. As a University Professor of English & Cultural Studies, Dr. Banerjee has taught and lectured in premier Universities across the globe in the USA,

UK, European, African and Asian countries and also recited her English Poetry & Indian Music at several Global Literary Festivals & International Conferences.

Rachel Bari, Ph.D. is a Professor of English and Director of Prasaranga, the publication division of Kuvempu University, and lives in Shimoga, Karnataka, India. Her latest publication is a book of poems titled *Body, Mind and Other Poems* published by Signorina Publications which came out in 2019. Her poems are also published in international anthologies like *Paradise on Earth* published by Third Eye Butterfly based in the US and *For You My love* by Indus Scrolls.

Arunima Bhattacharya, Ph.D. is Lecturer in English at Edinburgh Napier University. Her research interests include urban cultures, early twentieth-century travel literatures, island ecologies and fictions of the sea. She also has an active interest in museums and the heritage sector, particularly with community participation and co-creation. Her most recent work has been co-curating an intervention at the Hunterian Museum in the University of Glasgow titled, "Curating Discomfort" and co-editing and writing *Literary Capitals in the Long Nineteenth Century: Spaces beyond the Centres,* eds., Arunima Bhattacharya, Richard Hibbit and Laura Scuriatti (London: Palgrave, 2022).

Radha Chakravarty is a writer, critic and translator based in Delhi. Her poems appear in numerous journals and anthologies, including *Journal of the Poetry Society of India, Contemporary Major Indian Women Poets, Borderless, The Fib Review, Narrow Road Journal, Soul Spaces, Culture Cult, The Poet (Lockdown 2020), Krishna in Indian Thought, Literature and Music* and *Indian Poetry through the Passage of Time.* She has translated major Bengali writers including Rabindranath Tagore, and edited anthologies of South Asian writing. She contributed to "Pandemic: A Worldwide Community Poem" (Muse Pie Press, USA), was nominated for the Pushcart Prize 2020, and was nominated for the Crossword Translation Award, 2004. She taught Comparative Literature & Translation Studies at Ambedkar University Delhi.

Sangeeta Dey Roy hails from the hill station of Haflong, Dima Hasao, Assam. She is a teacher, poet, fiction writer and essayist, a member of the Intercultural Poetry and Performance Library (IPPL) and the Vice-President (Administrative) of the Indian Society for the Promotion of English Language and Literature (iSPELL).

Prathim-Maya Dora-Laskey teaches English Literature and Women's Studies at Alma College after graduate school on three continents. An alumna of Stella Maris College in Chennai, her awards include scholarships from the Pennathur foundation, the FSA board at the University of South Carolina, and a Violet Morgan Vaughan award at the University of Oxford. A poetry editor at *JaggeryLit Magazine* and a current moderator at SAWNET (south asian women›s net @ sawnet.org), she has published work in *Contemporary South Asia, Interventions: A Journal of Postcolonial Studies, South Asian Review,* and *Hypatia: A Journal of Feminist Philosophy.* Her poetry has previously appeared in *Yemassee, Mirror Magazine, Cerebrations, Eclectica Magazine, The Scriblerus Arts Magazine,* and a few anthologies. She can be reached at prathim.maya.doralaskey@gmail.com.

Tishani Doshi has published seven books of fiction and poetry, the most recent of which are a novel—*Small Days and Nights* (Bloomsbury), shortlisted for the RSL Ondaatje Award and a New York Times Bestsellers Editor's Choice, and a collection of poems, *A God at the Door,* shortlisted for the Forward Poetry Prize 2021. For fifteen years she worked as the lead dancer with the Chandralekha group in Madras, India. She is currently a visiting associate professor at NYU Abu Dhabi and otherwise lives in Tamil Nadu.

Pooja Garg is an award-winning writer having worked with India Today and is Founder of The Woman Inc (now South Asian Collective). She currently works as Deputy Editor for the Atlanta-based *Khabar* magazine. A USC Annenberg Fellow for DV Impact Writing and Community Storytelling, Pooja has been Poetry Editor for *Jaggery* and Open Road Review. Editor of *From My Window* Anthology, her poems have found a place in the *Best of 20 Years of Eclectica Poetry* and the *Red River Anthology* among other publications. Shabana Azmi called her poems "a must-read".

Shweta Rao Garg is an artist, poet, and academic from India living in Baltimore, US. Her poetry collection, *Of Goddesses and Women*, was published by Sahitya Akademi in 2021. She is one of the contributors to *Shakespearewalis: Verses on the Bard* (Flowersong Press, 2024). Her poems have been published in *Indian Literature*, *Coldnoon*, *Everyday Poems*, *Postcolonial Text*, *Transnational Literature*, *Muse India*, *Yugen Quest Review*, etc. Her poems are about her lived experiences as a woman and draw from Indian mythology and South Asian popular culture. Her artwork can be found at http://shwetaraogarg.com

Roopali Sircar Gaur, Ph.D., served as Associate Professor of English, Delhi University and Creative Writing at the Indira Gandhi National Open University. Her widely published poetry is archived in the Stanford University Pandemic digital archives. Dr. Roopali is an editor of several prestigious writing forums and has edited six international poetry anthologies. As Founder President of YUVATI a not-for-profit organisation for girls, she runs a special initiative called Mera Kitab Ghar: The Backyard Book Club. She has travelled extensively and is passionate about the welfare of military families. She lives in Meerut, India with her veteran husband and their three rescued dogs.

Anuja Ghimire is the author of four poetry books: two in Nepali Ankur and Arthaat, and two in English *Kathmandu* and *fable-weavers*. Her poems, stories, and essays have been anthologized and nominated for Best of the Net and Pushcart prizes, published in Nepal, India, Bangladesh, the U.S., Canada, the U.K., Scotland, and Australia. She works in the curriculum publishing industry. She is an associate editor for *Up the Staircase Quarterly*, newsletter editor for the Nepalese American Chamber of Commerce, and a judge for the annual essay writing contest for school children in DFW, organized by the Nepalese Buddhist Association. She loves conducting creative writing workshops for children in summer camps. She also volunteers for The Great Nepali Diaspora as the lead for the Creative Hub.

Bhaswati Ghosh writes and translates fiction, non-fiction and poetry. Her first book of fiction is *Victory Colony, 1950*. Her first work of translation from Bengali into English, *My Days with Ramkinkar Baij,* won her the Charles Wallace (India) Trust Fellowship for translation. Bhaswati's writing has appeared in several literary journals. *Nostalgic for a Place Never Seen* (Copper Coin, 2024) is her first poetry collection. She lives in Ontario, Canada. Visit her at https://bhaswatighosh.com/

Mandira Ghosh is an eminent poet, author, researcher and educator. She received the Author of the Year Award in 2022 from the Asian Literary Society, and the Bharat Nirman Award, amongst several other awards and honours. Published widely in India and abroad, she is the Guest Editor of Special Indian Edition of the *Seventh Quarry Swansea Magazine* from Wales and a recipient of a Senior Fellowship from the Ministry of Culture, Government of India. She is the treasurer of The Poetry Society India and also part of their Governing and Editorial Board She was the featured poet in the Seventh Quarry Swansea Magazine in April 2023.

Zerbanoo Gifford founded the charity, ASHA Centre (www.ashacentre.org) and was awarded the International Woman of the Year Award in 2006 for her humanitarian work. She is the author of seven books, including *Thomas Clarkson and the Campaign Against Slavery, Dadabhai Naoroji, Britain's First Asian M.P,* and *Confessions to a Serial Womaniser — Secrets of the Worlds Inspirational Women, which was* made possible by a NESTA Fellowship. Her memoir *An Uncensored Life* was published by HarperCollinsPublishers UK in 2015.

Nandini Guha is a retired Associate Professor of English from the College of Vocational Studies, University of Delhi. She received the Katha Award for translating Bani Basu's novel, *Dark Afternoons* (Katha, 2007) and won the Kalinga Literary Award for her translation of Bani Basu's *A Plate of White Marble* in 2021. Other translations from Bangla to English include Taslima Nasreen's autobiography, *Wild Wind* (Srishti Publishers, 2006) and Anita Agnihotri's, *Awakening* (Zubaan, 2009).

Renu Gupta is a Doctoral Researcher at the School of Business and Management at Queen Mary University of London. She applies her multi-disciplinary training towards her literary and social research; her work has been published by the *South Asian Review*. She writes predominantly in Hindi.

Dellnaz Wadia Italia works as a 'Design Aesthete' and a Stylist for her own Architecture and Interior Design firm based in Mumbai and Dubai. Her poems were published in an International Anthology titled *Impressions and Expressions: Anthology of Contemporary Poetry*, edited by the Oman-based poet Amita Sanghvi in 2021. She lives in Mumbai.

Jayshree Iyer has a doctorate in French literature from Tulane University with a specialization in medieval studies. Originally from India, she currently lives in New Hampshire, USA. She blogs at https://literarygitane.wordpress.com.

Zilka Joseph is an internationally published poet who has authored five collections. Her books were nominated, been finalists or won awards for PEN, Pushcart, and Notable Best Indie awards. Her work is influenced by her Indian and Bene Israel roots, and Western cultures. She was awarded a Zell Fellowship, the Michael Gutterman award, and the Elsie Choy Lee Scholarship from the University of Michigan. Her new book *In Our Beautiful Bones* is a Foreword INDIES finalist. Born and brought up in India, she now lives in Michigan, USA. She is a creative writing coach, manuscript advisor, and editor. Find her at: www.zilkajoseph.com

Soniah Kamal's most recent novel, *Unmarriageable: Pride and Prejudice in Pakistan*, a postcolonial parallel retelling writing back to Empire, was a 2020 Georgia Author of the Year for Literary Fiction nominee, shortlisted for the 2020 Townsend Award for Fiction, a *Financial Times* Readers' Best Book of 2019, a New York Public Library, NPR Code Switch and Library Reads picks and more. Soniah's work is in *The Georgia Review*, *The Bitter Southerner*, *The New York Times*, *The Guardian*, The Normal School and more. Her essays 'How to Survive Your Father's Imprisonment' and 'Writing the Immigrant Southern in the New New South' are Pushcart Prize nominees and her short story 'Jelly Beans' was selected for *The Best Asian Stories Series* 2017. Soniah is a Paul Bowles Fiction Fellow at Georgia State University where she earned an MFA in Creative Writing.

Amrit Kaur is a poet, storyteller, and communications professional who uses her words as a powerful weapon to bridge divides and create connections. A lover of literature, she has been writing and publishing creative work since a young age and was one of the founders of India's first PR and Communications company. With roots in three cultures—Punjab, Bengal, and Canada—she seeks to uncover the beauty and complexities of belonging and togetherness.

Ratika Kaushik holds a PhD from the University of Sussex in the field of postcolonial cultures. She is currently focused on research in the field of postcolonial cultures and gender studies. Her specialization includes diasporic studies, migrant narratives and the intersection of gender and nationalism. She works at NIIT, Neemrana as an Assistant Professor in the Humanities Department.

Hafiza Nilofar Khan is an Associate Professor in the Department of English and Modern Languages at the Independent University, Bangladesh. A recipient of the East West Center scholarship (Hawaii), and the PEO International Peace Scholarship (Iowa), Dr. Khan's researched articles, short stories, poems and translations are available on various sites. A Bangladeshi American born in Pakistan, and a mixed media artist, she speaks and dreams in multiple languages.

Sudipa Lama is from the small hill town of Mirik, located in the district of Darjeeling in West Bengal. An ardent advocate of the marginalized, she teaches in the Department of English at Mirik College.

Seetha Lakshmi is a queer Dalit woman from the southern part of India. They have a PhD in Social Work from Pondicherry University, and have been conducting LGBTQ+ research over the last five years. They also have an MPhil in Psychiatric Social Work from the National Institute of Mental Health and Neurosciences, and they believe in art as an instrumental tool of liberation.

Lalita Limbu is a youth feminist activist. Born and growing up in a marginalized Indigenous Community in the Eastern Part of the hilly region of Nepal, she has witnessed and experienced multiple levels of discrimination, suppression, and domination in the society. She holds a Master's in

English Literature and a Bachelor's in Law from Tribhuwan University, Nepal. She is currently working as a Program Associate at Bikalpa Gyan Tatha Bikas Kendra, Nepal, a non-profit movement-led organization. She is also engaged in mentoring young women and girls under the South Asian Young Women Leadership and Mentoring Initiative supported by the Global Fund for Women and CREA, India. Widely published, Banerjee has authored twelve solo books of poetry, along with several academic publications.

Shyamasri Maji is an Assistant Professor of English at Durgapur Women's College in Durgapur, West Bengal. She writes short stories and poems in English, some of which have been published in *Muse India* ("The Nettle Leaves"), *Six Seasons Review* ("Maya's Apartment"), *Story Mirror* ("The Birthday Party"), *Setu* ("Skin Poems"), *Kolkata Fusion, Café Dissensus, Indian Periodical, Borderless, The Chakkar, Teesta Review, Outlook India* and *Modern Literature*. She has read her poems at Anantha-Samyukta Poetry Festival and 'Humara Mushaira' of South Asian Literary Association, 2022. She may be reached at shyamasri.2010@gmail.com

Shikha Malaviya was born in the United Kingdom but grew up in the United States and India. Her family originally hails from Uttarakhand. Shikha's book of historical persona poetry, *Anandibai Joshee: A Life in Poems* is a unique retelling of the life of India's first female medical doctor and the first Indian woman to study medicine in the United States. Shikha's previous book of poems, *Geography of Tongues*, was published to acclaim in 2014. Her poetry has been nominated for the Pushcart Prize and featured in *Catamaran, PLUME, Prairie Schooner* & other fine publications. Shikha has been a featured TEDx speaker and was selected as Poet Laureate of San Ramon, California, 2016. Shikha is co-founder of The (Great) Indian Poetry Collective, a mentorship-model literary press and is currently a Mosaic America Fellow. She lives in the San Francisco Bay area with her family, where she is a poetry mentor, publisher, and workshop facilitator.

Kavita Ezekiel Mendonca has taught English in Indian colleges, AP English in an International School in India, and French and Spanish in private schools in Canada, in a career spanning over four decades. Her poems are featured in various journals and anthologies, including the *Journal of Indian Literature* published by the Sahitya Akademi and the *Yearbook of Indian Poetry in English*. Kavita has authored two collections of poetry, *Family Sunday and Other Poems* and *Light of The Sabbath*. She also enjoys writing nonfiction. Kavita is the daughter of the late poet Nissim Ezekiel.

Mary Anne Mohanraj is the author of *Tornado: A Breast Cancer Log, Perennial: A Garden Romance, A Feast of Serendib, Vegan Serendib, Bodies in Motion, The Stars Change*, and thirteen other titles. Other recent publications include stories for George R.R. Martin's *Wild Cards* series, stories at *Clarkesworld, Asimov's*, and *Lightspeed*, and an essay in Roxane Gay's *Unruly Bodies*. Mohanraj founded the Hugo-nominated and World Fantasy Award-winning speculative literature magazine *Strange Horizons*, and serves as Executive Director of both DesiLit (desilit.org) and the Speculative Literature Foundation (speclit.org). She is a Clinical Professor of fiction and literature at the University of Illinois at Chicago. www.maryannemohanraj.com

Mahvash K. Mohtadullah considers herself somewhat of a "serial corporate rut absconder", only because a sabbatical that was to last a year, has turned to eight and still sees no end in sight. Before that, she worked in the Financial Services Industry and was considered somewhat of a specialist process and experience "fixer upper". She began writing during the pandemic and has since published a collection of short stories, centring mainly around women of the larger Indian subcontinent, a book of poetry and essays, and two books in a children's series. Mahvash's stories and poems have appeared in *The Rumen, Sequoia Speaks, Recesses, PentaCat, Confetti, Every Day Fiction, Parcham, Blaze Vox and DoubleSpeak* magazines. Her poem, "Veins" was long listed in the Plough 2023 poetry competition. Her short story "The Glimmer" was long listed in the 2023 Zeenat Haroon Rashid writing competition for women.

Anita Nahal, Ph.D., CDP, is a Pushcart Prize-nominated Indian American author-academic. She has published four poetry collections; one of flash fiction, and four for children, as well as five edited anthologies. Her third poetry collection, *What's Wrong with Us Kali Women?* (Kelsay, 2021) was nominated by Cyril Dabydeen as the Best Poetry Book in 2021, and is included in the mandatory reading for a multicultural society course at Utrecht University. Her first novel, *Drenched Thoughts* came out in 2023. Anita teaches at the University of the District of Columbia, Washington, DC. She is the daughter of Sahitya Akademi award-winning Indian novelist, Late Dr. Chaman Nahal, and educationist Late Dr. Sudarshna Nahal. www.anitanahal.com

Shelly Naz is a Bangladeshi poet. She completed her Graduate studies in Zoology as well as International Community Development and is currently a PhD student in Australia studying patriarchy in Bangladesh, and the sexual commodification of the girl-child. She is a Deputy Director in the Ministry of Social Welfare, Government of Bangladesh. Naz has published nine poetry collections. Her published volumes of poems include: *Nakkhotro Khochito Danay Uddin Haremer Badi* [The Harem Slave Aloft on Star-Studded Wings] (2004), *Bishad Furey Jonmechi Bidyutlata* [An Electric Vine, | Pierced Through Sadness at Birth] (2006), *Shekoley Samudra Bajey* [The Sea Resounds in Shackles] (2007), *The Mummy and Sweetness* (2009), *Charjar Obadhyo Horini* [The Doe Disobedient to Rituals] (2009), *Shob Chabi Mithye Boley* [All Keys Lie] (2011), *Shucher Upor Hati* [I Walk on Needles] (2013), *Purushsamagra* [Male] (2015), and *Kata Jibher Gaan* [The Song of the Severed Tongue] (2021). Naz's poetry is feminist/confessional: She unmasks her personal experiences of patriarchy, and her verses manifest female sexual desire and deprivation which is largely unspoken in Bengali literature by female writers and poets. Her poetry has appeared in several anthologies and journals in Bangladesh and abroad, including in the UK, India, Nepal, and Ukraine.

Sophia Naz is a bilingual poet, artist, author, editor and translator. Nominated twice for the Pushcart Prize; in 2016 for creative nonfiction and in 2018 for poetry, her work features in numerous literary journals and anthologies. She has published several books of poetry: *Peripheries* (Cyberhex 2015), *Pointillism* (Copper Coin 2017) *Date Palms* (City Press

2017) *Open Zero* (Yoda Press 2021), and *Shehnaz*, a biography (Penguin Random House 2019). *Bark Archipelago* (Weavers Press, San Francisco & Red River India 2023) is her fifth collection of poetry.

Sunayna Pal, born and raised in Mumbai, now happily happily resides in Maryland with her family. Her poetry book, *Refugees in Their Own Country* (B&W Fountain) was published about the Partition of India. Her poetry has been published extensively in international journals and anthologies. She enjoys working as the Director of 'The Poetry Academy.' She is also devoted to the practice of Heartfulness meditation. Find more on her at sunaynapal.com.

Swati Pal, Professor and Principal, Janki Devi Memorial College, University of Delhi, has been a Fulbright Nehru fellowship awardee and a Charles Wallace and John McGrath Theatre Studies Scholar. Author of several books on theatre, creative and academic writing, her newspaper articles articulate her views on education. Her areas of research interest include performance studies and cultural history. She translates from Hindi to English. She writes poetry and her poems appear in several anthologies, two collections entitled *In Absentia* and *Forever Yours,* and an edited volume called *Living On*. She is the Vice Chair of the Indian Association for Commonwealth Literature and Language Studies and has been the recipient of several awards.

Suchita Parikh-Mundul works as a writer, copy editor and poet. Some of her articles on gender and culture can be read online at *The Swaddle*. Her poetry can be found in literary magazines like *The Bombay Literary Magazine*, Sahitya Akademi's *Indian Literature, Usawa Literary Review* and *Outlook India*. Her work has been included in various national and international anthologies. She lives in Mumbai, India.

Sonali Pattnaik, Ph.D. is an award-winning feminist poet, academic and visual artist. She is currently Visiting Faculty (Masters in English) and External Expert, Board of Studies in English at St. Xavier's College, Ahmedabad. She is the author of a book of poetry about surviving violence, resilience and love, *when the flowers begin to speak* (Writers Workshop 2021). Her poetry and art have been anthologised in *Of Brave Hearts* *and Dry Tongues* (Red River, 2022), *Through The Looking Glass* (Indie Blu(e), 2022), *The Kali Project* (Indie Blu(e), 2021) among others and published in journals including, *Muse India, Cafe Dissensus, Setu, Fem Asia* and *The Bombay Literary Review*.

Ayesha Perveen has a doctorate in English literature and works as an Assistant Professor at the Virtual University of Pakistan.

Nishi Pulugurtha is an academic, poet, and writer based in Kolkata. Her publications include a monograph on *Derozio* (2010), a collection of essays on travel, *Out in the Open* (2019), an edited volume of essays on travel, *Across and Beyond* (2020), a volume of poems, *The Real and the Unreal and Other Poems* (2020), a collection of short stories, *The Window Sill* (2021), and a co-edited volume of poems *Voices and Vision: The First IPPL Anthology* (2021). Her recent book is a volume of poems *Raindrops on the Periwinkle* published by Writers Workshop (2022). She is working on a book project that brings together recipes from the Telugu kitchen in Calcutta with tales of growing up in Calcutta/Kolkata. She also writes on Alzheimer's Disease. An edited volume of critical essays titled *Literary Representation of Pandemics, Epidemics and Pestilence* is forthcoming from Routledge.

Basudhara Roy teaches English at Karim City College, Kolhan University, Chaibasa. Author of three collections of poems, the latest being *Inhabiting*, she writes because she must test words on her tongue, pulse, moods, agitation, abstraction and satire. Her recent poetry is featured in the *Usawa Literary Review, EPW, Outlook, Live Wire, Madras Courier* and *The Dhakha Tribune* among others. She loves, rebels, overthinks, and reviews from Jamshedpur, Jharkhand.

Sumana Roy is the author of *How I Became a Tree*, a work of nonfiction, *Missing: A Novel, My Mother's Lover and Other Stories*, and two poetry collections, *Out of Syllabus* and *V. I. P: Very Important Plant*.

Shruti Sareen, born and brought up in Varanasi, studied at Rajghat Besant School, KFI. Graduating in English from Indraprastha College for Women, University of Delhi, she later earned a PhD from the same university. Her dissertation titled *Indian Feminisms in the 21st Century: Women's Poetry in English* was published in 2023 by Routledge (UK). She has also authored two monographs. Her debut poetry Collection, *A Witch Like You*, was published by Girls on Key Poetry (Australia) in April 2021. She has taught at Dyal Singh College, University of Delhi, and at Jamia Millia Islamia, another university in New Delhi. She may be reached at shrutanne.ipcollege@gmail.com.

Asha Sen is Professor of Postcolonial Literature and Grace Lau Senior Fellow at the University of Wisconsin-Eau Claire. She is the author of *Postcolonial Yearning: Reshaping Spiritual and Secular Discourses in Contemporary Literature* (Palgrave 2013), and numerous other publications. She loves books, dogs, films, and travel. Not always in that order.

Shafinur Shafin is a Bangladeshi poet, writer, translator, and academic. She is also the poetry editor of *Prachya Review*, an international literary webzine. Though her native language is Bangla, she also writes in English. Her first poetry collection, *Nisangam*, has been published in Bangladesh in 2016. Her poems and articles appeared in various national and international anthologies, magazines, and journals. She is currently pursuing her PhD at Universiti Brunei Darussalam. She can be contacted at shafinurnahar@gmail.com

Purvi Shah cultivates healing through anti-violence advocacy and creating art. She won the inaugural SONY South Asian Social Service Excellence Award for her leadership fighting violence against women. During the 10th anniversary of 9/11, she directed *Together We Are New York*, a community-based poetry project highlighting Asian American voices. Shah's most recent book, *Miracle Marks*, explores gender violence, racial inequity, and conundrums of the sacred. *Terrain Tracks*, her debut collection on migration and belonging, won the Many Voices Project prize. With Anjali Deshmukh, she creates interactive public art at https://circlefor.com/. Discover more @PurviPoets or http://purvipoets.net.

Dadoma Sherpa is a student at GP Koirala Memorial College pursuing a bachelor's degree in Business Studies.

Farah Siddiqui received a PhD in Literary Studies from The University of Texas at Dallas in Spring, 2022. She has an

MA in Communications from Notre Dame of Maryland University (2012) and an MA in English Literature from AMU (1997).

Jaspal Kaur Singh, Professor Emerita, English Department, Northern Michigan University, currently teaches at Oregon State University. Jaspal's book, *Exiles and Pleasures: Taunggyi Dreaming* received The Nicolás Cristóbal Guillén Batista Outstanding Book Award 2024, Caribbean Literary Association. Her books include *Violence and Resistance in Sikh Gendered Identity* and *Representation and Resistance: Indian and African Women Writers at Home and in the Diaspora*, among others. Her new book of fiction and memoir *Red Henna Blues* is forthcoming from Finishing Line Press in 2025.

Kalpna Singh-Chitnis is a Pushcart-nominated, award-winning, poet, writer, filmmaker and author of four poetry collections. Her works have appeared in *World Literature Today*, *Columbia Journal*, *Cold Mountain Review*, *California Quarterly*, *Indian Literature*, "Silk Routes "(IWP) at The University of Iowa, Stanford University's "Life in Quarantine," etc. Poems from her award-winning book *Bare Soul* and her poetry film *River of Songs* have been selected to go on the moon with NASA's missions in 2022 and 2023. A former lecturer of Political Science, she is also an Advocacy Member at the United Nations Association of the USA, and the Editor-in-Chief of "Life and Legends." *Website:* www.kalpnasinghchit-nis.com

Kashiana Singh strives to embody the essence of her TEDx talk - Work as Worship into her every day. Her chapbook *Crushed Anthills* from Yavanika Press in 2020 is a journey that unravels memory through 10 cities. Her latest full-length collection, *Woman by the Door* was released in Feb 2022 with Apprentice House Press. Kashiana lives in North Carolina and carries her various geopolitical homes within her poetry. Her poems have been published by *Rattle*, *Poets Reading the News*, *North Dakota Quarterly*, and *Beltway Poetry*, amongst others. (www.kashianasingh.com/)

Sukrita (Paul Kumar), a noted poet, critic and artist born in Kenya, has published several collections of poems, translations and critical books; her most recent collections of poems are *Vanishing Words* and *Dream Catcher*. An invited poet at the International Writing Programme (Iowa, USA) and a poet-in-residence in Hong Kong, she is a former Fellow of the IIAS, Shimla. A recipient of many fellowships and residencies, she held the Aruna Asaf Ali Chair at the University of Delhi. Currently, she is the guest editor of the journal *Indian Literature* and co-editor of "Writer in Context", a series of volumes published by Routledge UK.

Pramila Venkateswaran, poet laureate of Suffolk County, Long Island (2013-15) and co-director of Matwaala: South Asian Diaspora Poetry Festival, is the author of many poetry volumes, the most recent being *The Singer of Alleppey* (Shanti Arts, 2018) and *We are Not a Museum* (Finishing Line Press, 2022). She has performed her poetry internationally, including at the Geraldine R. Dodge Poetry Festival and the Festival Internacional De Poesia De Granada. An award-winning poet, she teaches English and Women's Studies at Nassau Community College, New York. She is the President of NOW Suffolk.

Vivimarie VanderPoorten teaches at the Open University of Sri Lanka. Her poem *Nothing Prepares You* won Sri Lanka's coveted Gratiaen Prize in 2007. She published two other collections, *Stitch Your Eyelids Shut* and *Borrowed Dust*. She also translates from Sinhala. Her work has appeared in *Postcolonial Text* and *Commonwealth's Adda*.

Rashna Wadia identifies as a Parsi-American writer and educator. Her work has appeared or is forthcoming in *Terrain. org*, *Yellow Arrow Journal*, *Salt Hill Journal* and others. She was the recipient of the 2020 poetry prize from *Kind Writer's Literary Magazine*. Rashna's work has been supported by VONA/Voices and Open Mouth. Currently, she is a poetry reader for *Chestnut Review*, and teaches in the San Francisco Bay Area.

Shernaz Wadia is from Pune, India. Shernaz's poems and articles have been published in many leading Indian and international e-journals, websites and print anthologies. She has published her own book of poems *Whispers of the Soul* and two volumes of *Tapestry Poetry*: *A Fusion of Two Minds* co-authored with her poetry partner Avril Meallem from Israel.

S.I. Welagedara (Shehani) is both a professional and amateur writer from Sri Lanka. Her day job includes drafting and polishing up all sorts of content. Her free time, on the other hand, includes communicating her thoughts through flowery words, metaphors and rhyme. When she is not writing, she prefers to get lost in reading or the latest book-to-screen adaptation. Shehani began writing back in 2009, and since then, the themes of her poems have expanded from cheesy romances and nature to feminism, gender and LGBTQIA+ rights.

Ather Zia, Ph.D., is a political anthropologist, poet, short fiction writer, and columnist. She is an Associate Professor of Anthropology and Gender Studies at the University of Northern Colorado. She is the author of *Resisting Disappearances: Military Occupation and Women's Activism in Kashmir*, Founder-Editor of *Kashmir Lit*, and co-editor of *Cultural Anthropology*.